T0128416

Musings *of a* Caribbean Professor

Dion E. Phillips

authorHOUSE®

AuthorHouse™
1663 Liberty Drive
Bloomington, IN 47403
www.authorhouse.com
Phone: 1 (800) 839-8640

Published by AuthorHouse 06/24/2019

ISBN: 978-1-7283-1450-1 (sc)
ISBN: 978-1-7283-1449-5 (e)

Library of Congress Control Number: 2019906484

Print information available on the last page.

This book is dedicated to
my faithful wife,
Maria Theresa Aguilar Phillips,
who has aided me vigorously
and constantly during
the twenty-nine years of our marriage

CONTENTS

IV

The Military of Barbados

V

Religion and Theology

X

Aging, Retirement and the Afterlife

PREFACE

As a university professor, though saddled with a perennially heavy teaching load and in later years, administrative chores – Chair, Department of the Social Sciences and Acting Dean, College of Liberal Arts and Social Sciences – I was nevertheless very conscious of the injunction "publish or perish."

The images of this quid pro quo come into play in the following anecdote. In response to the query "*who was he?*" two of the Roman soldiers that stood looking up to Jesus on the Cross responded with dissimilar answers. The first remarked: "They say he was a great teacher." The second soldier nodded wisely: "Yes, but he did not publish anything?" This is meant in jest since the Bible is one of the world's best sellers.

Robert and Jan Solomon, in the book Up the University: Recreating Higher Education in America (1983), alludes to this very point. "Once upon a time there was a philosopher named Socrates…He had some of the best ideas in the world. He was spectacularly witty and devastatingly smart. He would rather die than not talk philosophy." So, the Athenians killed him. Why did they kill Socrates?" He perished because he did not publish.

The articles that comprise the contents of this book which are titled Musings of a Caribbean Professor did not serve to avert my demise. With few exceptions, each of the over fifty entries were previously published in various newspapers in the Caribbean, particularly The Virgin Islands Daily News and *The* St. Croix Avis. Though submitted routinely as part of my annual evaluation or record of activities, they were reckoned under community service, rather than professional development, one example being a publication in a learned peer-review journal. The benefit of this book is that these articles are found here under one cover.

The democratization (or the making available for public consumption) of research work to The mass media and by extension to the public has been looked upon askance in the academy for ages. However, attitudes are changing and there is a narrowing of the gap between the town and the gown. This increasing recognition of the value of the popularization of research work or the dissemination of ideas in the ivory tower is beginning to take root. The articles in this work are a feeble attempt to link the streets with the academic elites.

Musings of a Caribbean Professor, part 2, is high on my mind. However, this is overshadowed by the sage advice of the late Robert Frost: "I leave a great deal to unfinished business."

Dion E. Phillips

ACKNOWLEDGEMENTS

I did not know that I would be a professor. I was initially trained to be a businessman and to follow in the footsteps of my father, Ernest Owen Phillips. Business did not gel with me, but I did not cast it aside. Looking back, it was my elder and only brother, Glenn Owen, a historian, who influenced my decision.

Having retired from the University of the Virgin Islands in 2017, after 35 years as a sociology professor in the academy, looking back, it was a good ride. When you find a job that you like, you will never have to work one day in your life.

However, it was far from being a solo contribution. My wife, Theresa; our son, Ernest Owen Nicandro and other family members, Mariette and Ret, including my only sister and the last of three siblings, Sonja Taylor, stood behind me.

My profound thanks is also extended to editors at the two leading newspapers in the United States Virgin Islands, namely, <u>The Virgin Islands Daily News</u> and <u>The St. Croix Avis</u>. Articles that were published in the foregoing sources and other outlets (<u>Barbados Advocate</u>, <u>Barbados Nation</u>, <u>Caribbean Contact</u>, <u>Jamaica Gleaner</u>, Dominica's <u>New Chronicle</u>, and Puerto Rico's <u>San Juan Star</u>) serve as the building blocks of this work. Hence, the book is a compilation of the newspaper articles that were published during my sojourn at the University of the Virgin Islands.

This is also an opportunity for the author to express his sincere gratitude to others who, in one way or the other, facilitated the writing of this book. I am highly indebted to Dr. Trevor B. Parris for his insightful and editorial efforts.

My gratitude to the Aguilar clan, particularly Oming and Ellen, for their logistic support in the production of the first draft on my fourth month-long visit to the Philippines in 2018.

To all of the foregoing and countless others, especially my esteemed colleagues, staff members (including Mary Dickinson and Diana Levons) and students at the University of the Virgin Islands and those beyond, whose association and support inspired me along the way, a million thanks!

And last but not least, a special thanks to The Almighty.

I

Outstanding Personalities

CYRIL E. KING AND THE VIRGIN ISLANDS IDENTITY

Caribbean Digest, Virgin Islands, vol. 6, no. 1, 1984: 17.

THE UNITED STATES Virgin Islands is a geographical area with a rich history of achievement, but it has relatively few monuments commemorating the heroes of the past. That is exactly why the September 18, 1984, decision of the 15th Legislature of the Virgin Islands to rename the airport in St. Thomas after the late Governor Cyril Emmanuel King is noteworthy. It points to a burgeoning Virgin Islands consciousness.

King was a Virgin Islander who deserves our honor. In 1949, he was appointed an aide to Senator Hubert Humphrey of Minnesota and was the first Black to serve on the staff of the U.S. Senate. He was also the second elected governor of the Virgin Islands, serving from 1975-78.

The decision to rename the airport in his name is not only conditioned by the fact that King, unlike past U.S. President Harry Truman after whom the airport was previously named, is a native Virgin Islander, but more importantly, because it was King himself who was responsible for getting the airport started.

King was a visionary. Although overzealous at times, he saw the need for a modern airport to serve the mono-economy of the U.S. Virgin Islands in the 1980's and beyond. King knew full well that the sole airport in St. Thomas, the tourist mecca of the tri-island territory, was the major gateway for the majority of the visitors to its shores and an important infrastructural component in the Virgin Islands' thrust toward economic development.

Interestingly enough, renaming the St. Thomas airport after a local hero is consonant with an emerging pattern in the Caribbean. The Norman Manley and Grantley Adams airports in Jamaica and Barbados, respectively, to name but two, have long since been re-named after prominent "sons of the soil." I may add, though, that the Coolidge airport in Antigua, named after U.S. President Calvin Coolidge, is an anomaly and points to the vestiges of neo-colonialism in a sovereign state.

Of course, it may be argued that the notion of honoring outstanding Virgin Islands leaders is a kind of narcissism and that any such personalities mentioned need no statues erected or anything of the kind in their memory. Rather, their achievements may be considered to be their monuments. However, past Virgin Islands Legislatures were not of this mind. Those already honored are Rothschild Francis, J. Antonio Jarvis, D. Hamilton Jackson, Lionel Roberts, Emile Griffith and so on.

In more recent years, the Virgin Islands has named a number of schools after prominent educators such as Eudora Kean, Edith Williams, Jane Tuitt and Arthur Richards. This is commendable, but it is not enough

The Virgin Islands need to rename streets and erect statuary, perhaps in the form of relief busts on the walls of halls, at entrances or other appropriate places. In doing so, let us remember those who have made contributions in medicine, dentistry, social services, the legal profession, labor and yes, even the often-forgotten enslaved.

In a land where many geographical areas are still referred to by such colonial names as "Estate Thomas" and "Sugar Estate," the decision to erect a statue of an anonymous and symbolic slave would serve to underscore the undisputed contributions of our fore-parents to Virgin Islands society and culture. Moreover, a society must have a sense of its past. There is no doubt that slavery has been a significant factor in our history.

We need reminders of where we started, how far we have come and what sort of mettle is characteristic of the Virgin Islands people. We need figures or monuments of our heroes so that we may be frequently reminded of the struggles that were necessary often against insuperable odds to bring these Virgin Islands to the level of freedom and development they enjoy today.

But the struggle is not over. We must consider that if we ignore the beacons of our past, the course of our future can be impaired. Let us, therefore, irrespective of budget constraints, re-evaluate our priorities and endeavor to erect visible mementoes of our heroes and heroines for posterity.

It behooves us to present our youth, our future leaders, with heroes and role models who are consonant with the ethos of our society and with whom they can readily identify. The erecting of statues and mementoes in public places to distinguish contributors to the Virgin Islands community should not be construed as a mere means of paying tribute to those contributors. They can also lend a certain style and a cachet to the physical environment, and more importantly, serve as a means of awakening a "national consciousness." With this is mind, the change in name of the St. Thomas airport was long overdue and Virgin Islanders deserve more of the same.

Sad to say, but we worship too much of that which comes from elsewhere. In the eyes of far too many Virgin Islanders, if a thing or a person is from abroad, it is supposed to be better than that which is indigenous. This attitude is myopic and self-defeating. We must create an ethos of self-integrity and collective worth.

Let us tell our children and our visitors of the achievements of Virgin Islanders. This is one instance of doing so, as in fact is the case with the renaming of the St. Thomas airport after the late Governor King. For in educating others, we educate ourselves. The airport is often the visitor's first and last points of contact.

TERENCE A. TODMAN: A FIRST-RATE PUBLIC SERVANT

VI Daily News, August 21, 2014: 6.

THE DEATH OF many a public figure often causes us to put certain aspects of that person's life in context. Like in some movies, the ending seems to illuminate the story line, bringing new significance to well known facts.

We pay no greater compliment than to acknowledge that U.S. Ambassador Terence Todman, a Virgin Islander and Caribbean man, will likely go down in the annals of history as one of the greatest United States public servants and as one who cared deeply about the region.

Though it has now become a routine for the United States President to pay an official visit and hold talks about matters of mutual interest with Caribbean Prime Ministers and other Heads of State, it was in 1977 that Rosalynn Carter, representing her husband, President Jimmy Carter, visited the Caribbean and the pattern was begun.

At that time, Todman served as Assistant Secretary of State for Inter-American Affairs (now Western Hemispheric Affairs). In fact, a Caribbean desk at the State Department was set up to address the concerns of small states, including push-button cases like Haiti.

This time also witnessed the heady Cold War days leading up to the Grenada Revolution, led by Prime Minister Maurice Bishop. Todman became the first U.S. diplomat in 16 years to visit Havana, Cuba.

Interestingly, after Carter left office, fellow Virgin Islander and former V.I. Governor Melvyn Evans served as U.S. Ambassador to Trinidad and Tobago at the time of U.S. military action in Grenada, under President Ronald Reagan.

Even after resignation, Todman returned to the diplomatic arena when he was named a special envoy by the Organization of American States (OAS) to promote democracy in Haiti during the Jean-Bertrand Aristide presidency.

Terence Todman's significant contribution to the Caribbean ought to be counted with his roles as Ambassador to Chad, Guinea, Costa Rica, Spain, Denmark and Argentina. It is reasonable to expect, and deservingly so, that historians will etch the sterling and stunning record of this great figure in the pages of time. They will likely conclude that he had a soft spot and a special eye for the Caribbean.

In paying tribute to Ambassador Terence A. Todman, we salute his wife, Mrs. Doris W. Todman, four children, including our colleague in the Social Sciences Department, University of the Virgin Islands, Dr. Patricia Rhymer Todman, and other members of the family. God will strengthen and guide you during your grief. May he rest in peace.

❖

Nelson Mandela Needs V.I. Support

VI Daily News, September 6, 1983: 6.

F EW OF US know him. His name is Nelson Mandela. He is a South African nationalist cum freedom fighter, involved in a struggle whose ultimate triumph will honor us all — the end of apartheid in South Africa.

There is often a thin line between a terrorist and a freedom fighter. It boils down to perspective. Both Menachem Begin and Anwar Sadat were freedom fighters, albeit terrorist for some, who rose to become chief executives in their respective countries of Israel and Egypt. And so, what bodes for Mandela? Will history absolve him?

Nelson Mandela is a South African patriot and a man of impeccable credentials. He is a descendant of the royal family in the Transkei; a graduate of Fort Hare University and the recipient of a law degree from Witwatersrand University.

Somewhat like Robert Bradshaw in St. Kitts/Nevis, Kwame Nkrumah in Ghana and Martin Luther King Jr. in the United States, Mandela chose to fight for the liberation of his people. The price has been costly.

As a consequence of the famous Rivonia treason trial in 1964, Mandela has been in prison for over 10 years. He was sentenced to life imprisonment in the maximum security prison called Robben Island.

Now, let us get things straight. South Africa is no joke place. Life imprisonment really means what it says. You are in prison until death removes you. The notion of benefiting from a commuted sentence is almost nonexistent. Moreover, the conditions on Robben Island are harsh and cruel and meant to break not only the spirit and body of its inmates, but also squelch the very cause that sent them there.

According to testimony given on oath to the United Nations Human Rights Commission, which investigated the conditions of prisoners and detained persons in South African jails, Robben Island is depicted as a prison with gross and inhuman conditions not fit for human habitation. There is little or no respect for the dignity and worth of the human beings incarcerated there.

Irrespective of the passage of time and the morbid and debilitating effects of Robben Island, Mandela has remained a symbol of African courage, tenacity and statesmanship. Surely you can destroy the human body; but it is infinitely more difficult to crush the human spirit. Ultimately, right is better than might, even though the latter may be in the ascendancy for the moment.

However, in real terms, the situation has not improved. Sad to say, Mandela's health recently has taken a turn for the worse and his sight is growing dim. These and other developments have led to recent talk and conjecture regarding the likelihood of Mandela's possible release and a reversal in the intransigent policy of the South African Government.

Mandela's prison release is contingent upon his willingness to desist from nationalist activities connected with the African Nationalist Congress (ANC). The ANC has long been labeled a racist and terrorist organization by the South African Government.

The irony of this allegation is that the ANC's leadership, including Chief Albert Lithuli, Mandela and others, has never predicated its case for political reform upon a platform of hate for, and vilification of, the whites in South Africa. Rather, the offensive of the ANC has always been buttressed by the application of the known principles of democracy and respect for the human being.

Mandela is one example of that kind of individual who, despite the odds, has dared to stay in South Africa and fight for justice, even to his own detriment. The outcome is no surprise. The South African apartheid regime, in spite of the chilly wind of international disapproval, has, in its own defense, set out to humiliate and liquidate all those African leaders who are perceived as threats to its authority.

There is no parallel in modern history for what is meted out to Mandela and to black people in South Africa. Conditions in that unhappy country represent the most monstrous, systematic and brutal denial of human rights to an entire people on the basis of race in the contemporary world.

The reprehensibility of such horror is not reduced by the embrace of the Ronald Reagan administration which argues that contact with the anti-communist Botha regime is meant to persuade the government to be more reasonable.

Mandela is an honorable man. So is the cause with which he is associated. Let us in the Virgin Islands not fail in our collective responsibility to give him and our brothers and sisters in South Africa the kind of support that will help them to withstand the pressures they face in their continuous struggle for social justice.

Garvey's Dream Still Alive

VI Daily News, December 14, 1983: 6.

MARCUS GARVEY WAS one of the most important leaders of the 20th century. Not only is he the father of modern Black Nationalism, but he is also a key pioneer in the Pan-African movement affecting the thought and practice of black leaders and the masses in Africa, the Caribbean and throughout the world.

Like all great dreamers, Marcus Garvey was a person ahead of his time as well as people's ability to understand the significance of his life's work. Although he died not having fulfilled his life's dream, the spirit of Garveyism still lives in the hearts of thinking people everywhere.

When Marcus Garvey founded his organization in Jamaica, he was rebuffed. His ambition was to establish a black nation. His theme, "Africa for the Africans at home and abroad", seemed ludicrous, but at the core was a commitment to win political, social and economic freedom for the world's Black people.

At the time the idea of self-determination for Blacks seemed far-fetched. Even the name he chose for his organization seemed preposterous – "United Negro Improvement Association."

As a consequence, Garvey received little initial support.

The black-skinned West Indians of the day were reticent to share his vision. In that era, Blacks were expected to "know their place" and most did.

Moreover, the light-skinned population opposed Garvey. Better placed in the social order of the British colonial bureaucracy than their black-skinned counterparts, the middle and mulatto classes favored nothing that would undermine their position in the Jamaican social structure of that time.

The cleavage among Blacks must be seen in the light of the fact that the general black consciousness associated with the 1960s was still a thing of the future.

But Garvey's dreams would not be easily defused. He was determined "that the black man would not be kicked about."

In 1916 he immigrated to the United States. Harlem's ghettos were fertile political soil for organization and in the racial tensions of those times, Blacks were ripe for the acceptance of a dynamic leader. It was the apt conjuncture of the man and the socio-economic times.

There were the usual vicissitudes. Nevertheless, Garvey brought hope to a sufficient number of the oppressed and the movement flourished. He claimed membership of over two million blacks.

Garvey developed one of the first formidable black newspapers in the United States. His weekly, "Negro World," was circulated around the globe in English, French and Spanish.

But the cutting edge of the movement was the "Black Star Line," a steamship company. This venture was intended to serve as a link to Black people everywhere. Shares were offered exclusively to blacks and Garvey received popular financial support.

This, however, proved to be his "Achilles heel." Neither he nor his organization were sufficiently knowledgeable about ships.

Mismanagement was excessive. Such a noble venture was therefore destined for failure.

In keeping with his unswerving commitment to black economic development, Garvey continued to sell shares to interested parties. Before long he was charged with fraud; subsequently convicted; sent to jail in 1927 and upon his release deported to Jamaica.

Upon return to his native land, Garvey continued to work assiduously for his dream of black nationhood. His U.S. jail term in Georgia had transformed him into a martyr for the cause of the black man. But he had long reached his zenith.

Factionalism developed within the movement and when Garvey was jailed in Jamaica for contempt of court, his prestige sank to an all-time low. With dwindling political support, he disappeared slowly from the public eye. In 1935, he moved to London where, five years later, he died.

Marcus Garvey never lived to see his dream come true. It was too ambitious for his time. But he awakened the consciousness of hundreds of thousands of Black people.

When he died, there were no post-World War II politically independent Black countries in Africa or the Caribbean. Ethiopia was the first independent member of the 20th-century League of Nations and retained its sovereignty from long-term colonialism. Liberia gained independence in 1847. However, in succeeding years, no less than 40 African and 10 Caribbean countries have moved on to independence or constitutional decolonization.

It is an irrefutable fact that the independence explosion in Africa and the Caribbean as well as the Black man's unprecedented confidence in himself in the world at large – continental U.S. and Virgin Islands included – have unquestionably had their genesis in Garvey's thoughts and practices.

Although this theme of Black unity remains unfulfilled, there is no question in the 1980s about the veracity of the spirit of nationalism that exists in predominately Black countries and among Blacks or African Americas in the United States.

Clearly this very spirit is evidenced today by the decision of Rev. Jesse Jackson to enter the presidential race and in so doing become the first black male U.S. presidential candidate (not forgetting Shirley Chisholm, the first woman to run for the Democratic Party's presidential nomination in 1972). In spite of the remote chance of victory, Jackson could make his presence felt in the 1984 contest.

Garvey's contribution to the liberation of Blacks and other dispossessed people cannot be overlooked. At his prompting and that of other outstanding thinkers, Black people in Africa, the Caribbean, the United States and other parts of the diaspora have only begun to redefine who they are as individuals and their own national identities.

Once this is accomplished, it may be that forward-looking Blacks in alliance with other non-Black progressive forces can, in due course, move to further alter the internal class structures in which they find themselves.

Garvey's dream, however incomplete, may be a dream delayed but not a dream deferred. Irrespective, it is a dream well worth our claim.

II

Caribbean and World Politics

Post-Cold War U.S.-Caribbean Relations

St. Croix Avis, May 9, 1997: 10; *VI Daily News*, May 16, 1997: 12;

The Sunday Gleaner (Jamaica), May 18, 1997: 8A & 10A; *San Juan Star (Puerto Rico)* May 23, 1997: 69;

The Labor Spokesman (St. Kitts and Nevis), 31 May 1997: 7.

U.S. President Bill Clinton arrives in Barbados today to attend a special summit with Heads of state and top-ranking ministers of the Caribbean having completed a tour of Mexico and Central America. This will be the second visit by a U.S. President to Barbados, the first being President Reagan in April 1982.

The event is expected to increase areas of cooperation and strengthen U.S.-Caribbean relations while seeking to harmonize common goals with respect to trade, economics and security issues. It is the last that has resulted in disagreement relative to the attempt of the U.S. to secure bilateral maritime drug interdiction agreements, better known as the "Shiprider." Such disagreements have invoked shadows of "recolonization."

The Caribbean has become the transshipment point for, by some estimates, 40 percent of all the cocaine and heroin destined for the United States. In December 1996, President Clinton added Aruba and the Netherland Antilles to a U.S. list of major drug-producing or drug-transiting countries. The Bahamas, Belize, Dominican Republic, Haiti and Jamaica are also listed. Two territories, namely, Puerto Rico and the U.S. Virgin Islands, from which drugs are allegedly easily shipped to the U.S. mainland have been dubbed "high-intensity areas."

The drugs have brought violence and the threat of corruption. Puerto Rico has a high murder rate and authorities say that 70 percent of the homicides are drug-related. St. Kitts and Nevis was rocked by a 1994 cocaine-slaying scandal involving three sons of the deputy prime minister, one of whom was murdered.

In the "war on drugs," there has been cooperation over the years between the U.S. Coast Guard, on the one hand, and those of the Caribbean and the Barbados-based Regional Security System, on the other. However, in seeking to strengthen the nexus, the U.S. lobbied area governments "one by one" to sign ship rider agreements which would allow unlimited surveillance of their air space and territorial waters.

Belize, the first to sign, did so in 1992. In the Eastern Caribbean, St. Kitts-Nevis was the first to do so on 13 April, 1995, almost a full year before Prime Minister (PM) Basdeo Panday signed the Trinidad and Tobago (TT) version when Secretary of State Warren Christopher visited the state in March 4, 1996. Prior to TTs signature, agreements were completed with Antigua-Barbuda, Dominica, Grenada, St. Lucia, St. Vincent-Grenadines as well as the Dominican Republic. In the case of the Bahamas, its bilateral partnership with the U.S. which is reputed to have resulted in a reduction of trafficking, dates back to 1985.

Nevertheless, several of these countries reported pressures from the U.S. to sign. Barbados and Jamaica who both finally acceded to a much revised text, initially balked and called for fresh dialogue which resulted in a cooling of hitherto warm relations with the U.S.

Barbados' PM Owen Arthur, in a speech in Trinidad, likened U.S. action to the Brezhev Doctrine of "limited sovereignty that led to the subjugation of Eastern Europe on the grounds that they could not provide for their own defense." This notion is akin to Elliot Abrams' call for some Eastern Caribbean countries to give up some of their sovereignty in exchange for U.S. protection and assistance.

According to him in an article in <u>The National Interest</u>, such ideas are premised on the view that "small Caribbean states are inherently non-viable and will tend toward instability." Hence, the U.S. should be an "activist in the Caribbean backyard" since migration from the region and drug transiting constitutes a threat to U.S. interest. There have been more than 100,000 drug-related deaths in the U.S. in the 1990s, and so, the relocation of the Southern Command from Panama to Miami which is scheduled to take responsibility for the Caribbean Sea on June 1, 1997, appears to be part of the U.S. post-Cold War strategy.

Others feel, including Ivelaw Griffith, author of <u>Drugs and Sovereignty in the Caribbean</u>, that in an age of global interdependence, the concept of sovereignty might require a redefinition. And so, though Caribbean leaders may not wish to be seen to be bowing to U.S. dictates, possibly one of the legacies of the Grenada invasion in 1983, they should face up to the reality that they, individually and/or collectively, have serious limitations which prevent them from effectively tackling the drug dealers and that the U.S. has the greatest capacity to be helpful in the drug war.

We will have to wait and see what will be the concrete outcome of this U.S.-Caribbean Summit beyond its obvious "symbolic importance" as Caribbean leaders attempt to link security concerns to general development issues, whether drugs, trade or economic relations, is a more advantageous approach.

One thing that the region's leaders may have already learned, particularly the more pliant ones, is that in external relations, instead of being picked off "one by one," a coordinated and collaborative approach to international issues – whether drugs, trade or economic relations – may very well be a more prudent approach.

--- ◆ ---

China's Presence across the Caribbean
VI Daily News, June 23, 2016: 22.

C HINA IS POSITIONING itself to be an increasingly influential actor
in a distant world – the Caribbean – that has traditionally been
attached to its principal rival, the United States.

Already, the British Virgin Islands is a leading destination for mainline
Chinese overseas direct investment, along with Hong Kong and the
Cayman Islands.

The U.S. Virgin Islands may yet be drawn into its vortex on account
of the recent exploratory visit of the Governor of the Virgin Islands,
Kenneth Mapp.

China's remarkable economic expansion has raised eyebrows across the
globe, and the Caribbean is no exception. Once largely absent from the
region, the People's Republic of China (PRC) has emerged in recent years
to become both a competitive threat and an important economic partner.

Since former Chinese Premier Jiang Zemin's landmark visit to the region
in 2001, successive delegations of Chinese and Caribbean officials have
signed trade and investment deals, economic cooperative pacts and
discussed security concerns.

China's Caribbean engagement reached new heights with the three-day
state visit to Trinidad and Tobago by President Xi Jinping in June 2013.

This strategy of engagement is intended to ensure region-wide support for a "One-China policy"; utilize the Caribbean to increase China's global market share as an exporter, and assist with energy security, which accounts for its specific interest in Trinidad and Tobago, Jamaica and Guyana.

Be it diplomatic missions, aid/or trade, the issue of Taiwan remains at the core. Since official United Nations recognition in 1971 and U.S. President Richard Nixon's landmark visit to the People's Republic of China (PRC) one year later, Caribbean and Latin American countries, with some exceptions, increasingly have diplomatically recognized the PRC over the Republic of China (Taiwan), as representative of the Chinese people.

Prior to 1970, China's ties with the Caribbean were heavily weighted on its ideological connection with Cuba, which recognized Beijing as early as 1960.

In addition to Cuba, the PRC is now recognized by nine Caribbean countries: Antigua and Barbuda, Bahamas, Barbados, Dominica, Guyana, Jamaica, St. Lucia, Suriname and Trinidad and Tobago. Diplomatic relations between the English-speaking Caribbean region was begun by Guyana in June 1971, followed by Jamaica in November of that year.

The region has witnessed defections to China over the last two decades, some of which have reverted back and forth, but today only five Caribbean countries continue to recognize Taiwan: Belize, Dominican Republic, Haiti, St. Kitts and Nevis, and St. Vincent and the Grenadines. With five of the fifteen Caribbean countries that still have diplomatic ties with Taiwan, the Caribbean region represents a strategic knot that Beijing eventually would like to further unravel.

Trade with China is largely one-way. Loan commitments and assistance to countries mainly for construction – sports stadiums, highway construction, port facilities and other infrastructural projects, including in the tourism industry – employ a majority of Chinese workers at a time of high unemployment in Caribbean countries, provide no knowledge transfer, and increase debt levels.

The prime minister of Barbados, Freundel Stuart, did raise with President Jinping, on the occasion of the first visit of a president of China to the Caribbean, the need to improve China's imports so as to redress the considerable surplus in favor of trade between China and the Caribbean.

There has also been cooperation in the field of culture, sports, tourism, health and education. Students study in China as a result of Chinese government scholarships. There are Confucius Institutes at the University of the West Indies, both at the Mona and St. Augustine campuses, Jamaica and Trinidad.

Though Haiti is one of the few countries in the world that recognizes Taiwan in continued opposition to the mainland's "One-China" policy, the People's Republic of China (PRC) contributed forces to the Brazilian-led, Haitian-based peacekeeping force in 2004 in the form of a detachment of the Popular Liberation Army (PLA) security police.

This marked the first significant Latin American military or political presence in the circum-Caribbean region. Since that deployment, the force presence has been sustained, facilitated by troop rotations.

Also, several PLA and other officials were killed in Haiti's devastating January 2010 earthquake, becoming the first PRC military ranks to die officially in a Latin American/Caribbean territory in modern times. Then again, in September 2011, the Caribbean was chosen to be the destination of the PRC's first-ever military hospital ship to visit the Western Hemisphere. Notwithstanding, the United States still regards the Caribbean as its "Third Border" and will likely continue to guard against the presence of any major power because of its geopolitical security interests.

Though ties have been established with the military or security forces of the Caribbean, another social-oriented Grenada is not in the cards.

China appears to be limiting its substantive military activity to Asia and South-East Asia which it regards as its theater of interest.

China's interest in the Caribbean is intended to influence political decision-making on international issues like Taiwan and Tibet as well as garner support against a permanent seat on the United Nations Security Council for Japan. China's other interests are economic – access to minerals, oil, gas and forestry in such countries as Jamaica, Guyana and Trinidad and Tobago.

Along these lines, Beijing likely views the Caribbean as strategically important in view of its proximity to the United States, major maritime trade routes and infrastructure, such as the Panama Canal and the region's ports.

China's loans and private investments in projects give it political influence with the borrowing Caribbean countries and provides a return on its investments.

Never mind the often disconnect over imported Chinese labor practices, on account of the mutual benefits for the Caribbean and China, that country will likely expand its ties resulting in a strong and unique footprint.

For V.I. and Caribbean, Cuba is a Mixed Blessing

VI Daily News, December 23, 2014: 25.

T<small>HE</small> M<small>ONROE</small> D<small>OCTRINE</small> – the right to oppose foreign powers in the Western Hemisphere - named after its creator, President James Monroe in 1823 - was buried at the end of the cold war in the early 1990s, when the Berlin Wall fell and the Soviet Union collapsed. It left the United States without an arch enemy. However, it lingered on in the United States' continuing isolation of Cuba. Now, with the recent proposal of the Obama administration to restore diplomatic relations severed 50 years ago and open an embassy in Havana, what remains of the Cold War continues to wind down.

The world at large opposes the illegal and decades-old U.S. Blockade of Cuba: the U.N. General Assembly voted 188 in favor, 2 against (U.S. and Israel) and 2 abstentions on October 28, 2014. Though there is almost global condemnation of the U.S. for maintaining the blockade, it will remain on Cuba for now, though Obama plans to ease economic relations through executive order and call on Congress to go further.

Obama's policy toward Cuba appears to be the biggest difference of all the intervening presidents going back to President Dwight Eisenhower, many of whom tended to impose sanctions. Sanctions on Cuba are tighter than those against other U.S. adversaries such as Iran and Russia, although the U.S. does send food and medicine to the island when the humanitarian need arise.

Both the countries of President Obama and President Raul Castro have apparently agreed to put aside years of hostility, including the Cuban Missile Crisis of October 1962 which took the world to the brink of a nuclear war. In so doing, Obama wishes to put to an end, as he puts it, the "outdated approach that for decades has failed to advance our interests."

Caribbean countries who begun in 1972 - with Guyana, Trinidad and Tobago and Barbados - to stop the isolation of Cuba, by forming diplomatic relations, hailed the news of the shift in U.S.-Cuban relations though with a double-minded stance, and might have breathed a sigh of relief upon learning that the door will not be open wide for U.S. tourism on the Caribbean island, though that may only be a matter of time.

Mariel, in northern Cuba, has now become a major transshipment port in anticipation of the widening role of the Panama Canal. Cuba is angling for Mariel to become the major transshipment port in the Caribbean, connecting the Caribbean, Latin America, Asia, and beyond. Also, while Mariel is expected to become a free zone, the old shipping port at Havana is to be transformed and modernized to become a magnetic tourist port and destination. The capitol city will also serve as a cultural center and handle other business projects. American and other businesses are eager to benefit from these new initiatives.

With the end of the embargo looming on the horizon. Caribbean leaders should be careful for what they wish because the tourism-dependent economies of the region stand to suffer the most in terms of loss, particularly tourism traffic.

When that time comes, partnership with Cuba's tourism sector and the possibility of multiple-destination marketing may be one way to buffer the lost.

Guyana-Venezuela Dispute
Needs Diplomacy
VI Daily News, July 23, 2015: 27.

Back in 2005, a number of Caribbean countries, initially 12, including Guyana, the home of CARICOM's headquarters, gleefully signed the PetroCaribe agreement to lessen their strategic dependence on Washington and its various satellites such as the IMF and the World Bank.

The impact of the recession on the Caribbean was cushioned by the financial buffer provided by the PetroCaribe Agreement.

The PetroCaribe Loans Act, which allowed these Caribbean countries to receive Venezuelan oil at preferential rates, was an initiative of the late President Hugo Chavez, a man with regional leadership aspirations. Chavez's intention was to counter American hegemony in the region and to buy influence within the Anglophone Caribbean, indeed, the South as a whole.

After Chavez, who died in 2013, was replaced by his mentee, Nicolas Muduro, Caribbean leaders waited with baited breath to see whether Chavez's successor would continue to support Caracas's "PetroCaribe fund and other aid facilities" from which these cash-strapped and debt-burdened countries benefited enormously, except of course Barbados, Trinidad and Tobago, and Montserrat, which are not signatories. The fund is still intact but the chickens may be coming home to roost now that Maduro issued the Maritime agreement, May 26, 2015, laying claim to the Atlantic waters off the Essequibo coast of Guyana.

The last inkling of things to come occurred as recently as two years ago, October 2013, when the Venezuelan navy seized and detained a seismic survey or oil exploration vessel operating in the Essequibo under a Guyanese concession. It should therefore have come as little surprise that the discovery of a significant reserve of high-quality crude potential by Exxon Mobil Corp in that very region - the waters off the Essequibo - would trigger Venezuela's demand that Guyana halt the operation, thus making light of the 1899 agreement which called for Venezuela to relinquish claim to the Essequibo - an undeveloped but resource-rich jungle territory - that constitutes about two-thirds of Guyanese territory, 83,000 square miles.

It has long been felt that the 1899 Arbitration Award did finally settle the territorial dispute between Guyana and Venezuela and that both sides were bound to accept the decision. Both parties did until 1962 when strange circumstances intervened to cause Venezuela to reject, at the United Nations, the long-settled dispute.

Venezuela's position is that the 1899 ruling was invalid and questions its finality, and that it has many official maps that describe the Essequibo as Venezuelan territory. Guyana says that Venezuela pledged to abide by the ruling but later reneged. In the intervening years, apart from the skirmishes that were settled by diplomacy, differences were submerged and put to the side.

However, President Maduro's recent maritime May 26 decree may have laid bare the true intent of PetroCaribe as self-serving: the annexation of the territory from Guyana through insincere means. If nothing more, it shows that Venezuela's friendship with Guyana and CARICOM as expressed in the Petro-Caribe agreement is superseded by what it perceives as its vital interests, namely, the economic value of the Essequibo.

What underscores this view is that the May decree, which was issued soon after Guyana's announcement of a discovery of new reserves off the Essequibo coast, extends Venezuela's territorial claims further out into the Atlantic to encompass the area where the new discovery was made.

Guyana and its CARICOM partners object to the May decree, though the communique to that effect at the recently concluded July 2015 Heads of Government conference in Barbados, at which President Maduro was a no-show – he sent his deputy instead – was half-minded and failed to squarely address the issue.

At the same time, Maduro's posture is blunt. He has recalled the Venezuelan ambassador to Guyana for consultation and initiated a review of the relationship with Guyana, including a reduction of the size of the embassy staff there. This can be viewed as theatrics meant to divert attention from the reportedly failing economy, inflation and a spiraling homicide rate as well as Maduro's falling job approval rating and to rally nationalist sentiments around him in the upcoming elections.

Needless to say, the May decree has left the Caribbean countries living by their wits in they dealing with Venezuela. Their reality is: "Give me aid and I will be effectively silenced or left to perform the balancing act in the interest of my own survival."

The PetroCaribe agreement, invaluable as it is for the Caribbean countries, has placed them in the unenviable position of being beholden to Venezuela— not wanting to disrupt their relationship with the "giver of good gifts" but at the same time having the need to support Guyana, a fellow-CARICOM state.

If Maduro hunkers down, as implied by the most recent issuance of Venezuela ID cards to Essequibians to make them citizens, Guyana's territorial integrity and sovereignty will come under further assault. It is without the military resources to directly stop Venezuela. Collective security will prove to be the only effective and formidable defense against the travails of Venezuelan aggression.

Guyana's way forward is to internationalize the issue of Venezuela's threat of encroachment on its territory by invoking the relevant mechanisms of the various international organizations to which Guyana belongs, including the Organization of American States and the United Nations.

For small states like Guyana, diplomacy, not war, is the way forward.

◆

WILL NEVIS SECEDE?

VI Daily News, October 10, 1996: 14; *Caribbean Week,* November 9-22, 1996: 7.

New Chronicle (Dominica), Nov. 1, 1996: 36

POLITICAL OBSERVERS ACROSS the Caribbean are watching closely to see whether or not Nevis will secede from the 13-year-old St. Kitts-Nevis Federation. Nevis Premier Vance Armory made the threat in June following a disagreement with the Central Government in St. Kitts.

Nevisians are largely a friendly, independent-minded and proud people. This collective psyche may in part stem from the fact that the island was once the seat of government of the British West Indies. The governor general of the West Indies once lived there.

In 1882, when the British abolished the government in Nevis and linked or annexed it to St. Christopher (more popularly known as St. Kitts or "Sugar City" to many), Nevisians expressed their dissatisfaction with the decision by rioting.

In the ensuing years, the peoples of both islands, which together have a population of 52,500 and total 104 square miles, have since learned to restlessly accommodate one another, though from time to time there have always been rumbling about a possible separation.

Anguilla, located hundreds of miles away from St. Kitts and once a member of the three-island state of St. Kitts-Nevis-Anguilla, went its separate way in 1967. The remaining two, just about two miles away – between Mosquito Bay and Nags Head – and with a significant number of Nevisians having close relatives living in St. Kitts, have tended to coexist and tolerate each other.

However, this social arrangement is not immutable. So much so, that in September 1983 when St. Christopher and Nevis achieved independence, the last of the Commonwealth Caribbean countries to do so, its federal constitution made provision for the secession of Nevis as long as it was supported by a two-thirds majority in the Nevis parliament and by the population at large.

It may well be that the impulse of the people of Nevis to be free is coming to the surface and that these feelings are expressed in the secession bill which was read in the Nevis Island Assembly on 18 July, a measure that is reported to have received unanimous support.

A date for the forthcoming referendum has not yet been set, but it is believed in some quarters that secessionist sentiments are strong among some sections of the population.

Opponents of secession contend that Amory's popularity and that of his party, the Concerned Citizens Movement, which currently control 3 of the 5 seats in the Nevis Island Administration, have waned and that the secession drive is a diversionary tactic to rally support in their bid to regain the government in local Nevisian elections which are due on or before June next year.

To many onlookers, the idea of an independent nation of Nevis, thus leading to the further political fragmentation of the Caribbean, seems ludicrous not merely in view of the small or rather tiny size of the island and one with limited resources but, more so, at a time when there are clear trends in the Caribbean (of which Nevis is a part) and globally, toward regional integration.

However, the emotional impulse of a people to be free, as perceived by them and by its very nature, is often not based on logic and therein lies the dilemma.

Obama and Caribbean Policies

VI Daily News, November 6, 2008: 14.

P RESIDENT-ELECT OBAMA'S VICTORY could be bitter and sweet for
the Caribbean if the U.S. lifts the Cuban embargo.

Most residents of the Virgin Islands – including the governor and the
delegate to Congress, who had a change of heart – publicly endorsed
Barack Obama to replace George W. Bush. President-elect Obama will
imprint his stamp on U.S. foreign policy toward the Caribbean and the
world.

The irony of this moral support, since the right to vote for the presidency
has not been extended to US territories, is that the Virgin Islands and
Caribbean economies could suffer if Obama – who said the United
States should talk to estranged foreign leaders – decides to lift the
40-year embargo on Cuba. Last week, the United Nations General
Assembly voted for the 17th straight time to remove the embargo. In
that 192-member world body, only three countries voted no – the U.S.,
Israel and Palau. Cuba's Foreign Minister Felipe Perez Roque, quoted
in the Associated Press, "(I) expect the new president will change the
policy toward Cuba."

Also, the International Monetary Fund has forecasted that if the US
embargo is removed from Cuba, a mere 90 miles from Florida, that
island will see an increase of between 2 percent to 12 percent in stopover
visitor arrivals.

If this holds true, such an eventuality could have dire consequences for Caribbean tourism destinations, including the Virgin Islands that are heavily dependent on the U.S. market. One likely scenario is that it could result in a loss of market share, impact visitor spending and add hurt to the injury that is anticipated from the US economic crisis by increasing unemployment.

There may be another and bitter side to the euphoria of Obama's victory for Caribbean tourism if the US lifts the Cuban embargo. One of life's dilemmas is that we cannot always eat our cake and have it too.

III

Power and Politics in the Virgin Islands

V.I.'s Role in the Caribbean Basin Initiative

VI Daily News, August 17, 1984: 6.

For some time now there have been straws in the wind concerning the probable role of the U.S. Virgin Islands territory in facilitating the United States in its foreign policy toward the mini-states of the Eastern Caribbean.

This scenario was aired by Delegate to Congress Ron DeLugo in his address at the Reichhold Center when Eugenia Charles, prime minister of Dominica, visited the Virgin Islands at the invitation of the Caribbean American League on March 17, 1954.

Charles, on that occasion, in her capacity as the then-leader of the Organization of Eastern Caribbean States said that, irrespective of the flag flown in the Virgin Islands, "we must come close together as a united Caribbean region."

In another time and place, Ronald Mapp, the then Barbados ambassador to the United Nations, was of the same mind and envisioned a future Virgin Islands role in Caribbean affairs.

To all appearances, these statements are more than mere political imaginings. A pattern has begun to emerge.

Reagan's invitation to Gov. Juan Luis to join 27 other Caribbean heads of state at a three-day conference at the University of South Carolina in July as well as the inclusion of Henry Wheatley, de Lugo's aide, as a member of the congressional committee that visited the strife-torn Grenada underscores the fact that the idea of a meaningful role for the Virgin Islands in the U.S.-Caribbean relations is gaining momentum under the present administration.

Luis' visit with Reagan and other Caribbean leaders came on the heels of a bill that was passed in Congress with bipartisan support designating the College of the Virgin Islands as the home of the Eastern Caribbean Center, a cultural and scientific outpost to serve the vital socio-economic needs of the sub-region.

Some proffer that the center will be modeled after the East-West Center in Hawaii. Irrespective, the center could become part and parcel of the Caribbean Basin Initiative (CBI), the Reagan's administration's best and last hope for the Caribbean.

The CBI was proposed by the Reagan administration in April 1982. However, to date, many of the touted benefits are long in coming and Caribbean leaders, although hopeful, are becoming restless and impatient.

Edward Seaga, Jamaica's prime minister and Reagan's best friend in the sub-region, has long since stated that the problems of the area are deserving of a mini-Marshall Plan.

St. Lucia's John Compton, one of the Caribbean leaders, who along with the United States participated in the October 1983 invasion of Grenada, has recently echoed: "Our problems are not military but social and economic."

With this in mind, it is felt that the U.S. Virgin Islands, the only English-speaking American territory in the Caribbean, because of its involvement in testifying before key committees of the U.S. Congress, are strategically located to bring the viewpoint of the Caribbean nations to the policy makers in Washington.

Reagan's appointment of Thomas Anderson to replace Milan Bish as the new U.S. ambassador to Barbados and the other sovereign states of the Eastern Caribbean is in keeping with this pressing need. Anderson is reputed to be most familiar with the workings of the U.S. federal government, having spent 12 years of his life on Capitol Hill.

Unspeakably, the notion of the U.S. Virgin Islands developing closer ties with its neighbors in the Eastern Caribbean is a noble idea and one that is long overdue.

No stone should be left unturned to ensure that any such effort of mutual cooperation is consummated. Neighbors should always get to know each other better. It is a sad commentary that it took the Grenada tragedy to lead us down this path. Suffice it to say that out of crisis can come opportunity.

However, I offer one word of caution. Under the rubric of the CBI, much is reported to be at stake for the Eastern Caribbean, the U.S. Virgin Islands and the College of the Virgin Islands as well. Such reports have contributed to rising expectations.

However, it must be borne in mind that authentic U.S. Virgin Islands-Caribbean relations should emerge from the will of the people and not be imposed by some extra-regional source.

Caribbean solidarity as well as its much-needed socio-economic advancements can never be achieved as a by-product of any one's foreign policy, including that of the United States, however well-intentioned. For this reason, it behooves both Virgin Islanders and our Eastern Caribbean neighbors to be ever vigilant.

Poverty and Politics in the V.I.

VI Daily News, December 18, 1986: 6.

G ONE ARE THE days when the U.S. Virgin Islands could be characterized as "an effective poorhouse," as it was when President Hoover visited in 1931. These scenic islands have come a long way on the road to economic and social development.

It is commendable that the per capita income of the tri-island territory is among the highest in the hemisphere. However, according to sociologist Eddie Donoghue's Nov. 20 Daily News article, "Social Polarization in the V.I.," this truth does not tell the full story.

In a democratic-type society like ours, it is expected that a reasonable amount of benefits — of economic growth — will trickle down to the masses; however, if the 1980 census is a reliable source, the trickle is, at best, a very slow drip.

The statistics laid out by Donoghue are illuminating and astounding. Among other things, he states that in the indisputably affluent V.I. society, 37.1 percent of the black population as compared to 13.3 percent of whites live at or below the poverty line.

Such conditions of glaring racial inequality are fertile political soil for a populist leader. Moreover, they explain in large measure why the Independent Citizens Movement candidate Adelbert Bryan, who presented himself as the champion of the dispossessed, not only won enough votes in the general election to force Alexander Farrelly into a runoff but was able to claim a solid 35 percent of the vote in spite of the well financially oiled political machine of his principal opponent.

Unquestionably, the 2-1 margin of victory has given the Farrelly-Hodge team a clear mandate to administer the territory's affairs for the next four years. But if, in the interim, there is a lack of sober, observable attempts to address and redress the plight of "the small man," the next gubernatorial election could be the most divisive in the V.I. history.

Unattended poverty in the face of wealth is often an omen of things to come. The destitution associated with "absolute poverty" as found in places like Haiti does not exist here. But "relative poverty" is an integral part of the social fabric of V.I. society.

Such poverty is related more to expectations and to obvious stark contrast in living conditions or life chances. If a segment of society evinces an appreciable rise in the standard of living while another sector remains at a standstill, or only slightly improves its condition, the latter section must be considered for all practical purposes as relatively poor. Regardless, they subjectively see themselves as poor and that counts.

Apart from the fact that there is a rich, upper class here, I do not concur with Donoghue that there is no appreciable middle class. In fact, I agree with James Pobicki's Dec. 1 letter to the editor on one point, namely that there "have been gains shared by both blacks and white households" and a resultant middle class.

Its power, however, must not be misconstrued because of the non-classical nature of this grouping. The importance of such a class lies in its access to the state apparatus.

This new elite of politicians, bureaucrats and educated persons, many of whom are native black islanders, interlock with the media and business persons and is eager to define its status as was so aptly portrayed by the exercise of Bizpac in the recent elections.

It is logical and predictable that an extant middle class will seek to protect itself when it perceives its interest to be endangered. Hence, the middle class in the V.I. plays a significant and pivot role.

It serves as a buffer between the verifiable poor and an upper class. This, in large measure, explains why the Virgin Islands, in spite of the state of relative impoverishment, has been able thus far to avoid deep social friction and extremes in political polarization.

And so, though the Bryan/Sprauve team found a respondent chord among those who feel deprived of the benefits of the boom years, it lacked the financial clout and was outmatched by the organizational savvy of the more experienced Farrelly-Hodge combination.

V.I. poverty should not only be cast in sociological terms. There is also "case poverty" which often results from physical and mental disability or some vice.

The successful management of one's life requires a modicum of discipline and sobriety. The absence of these qualities will likely predispose persons to failure. Some among us will tend to squander their substance with riotous living.

So it is always tempting for the better-off in society, many of whom have pulled themselves up by their bootstraps, to explain away poverty by reference to individual inadequacies and self-inflicted wounds.

Though there is evidence of those who have been trapped in a cycle of welfare dependence and have tended to make a convenience of their situation, the proclivity to blame the victim without providing optimum opportunity for upward mobility incurs a sense of shame, and leads to greater resentment.

The poor may come to feel, not altogether wrongly, that one man's wealth may be the direct cause of another's impoverishment. The Rastafarian ideology is replete with this kind of socio-political thinking.

The '86 election testifies to the fact that Virgin Islanders have become caught up in the syndrome of rising expectations. Given the wide disparity in wealth, there is now a rising tide of discontent. A sizeable number of voters, still a minority, seemingly no longer regard the present character of social polarization as acceptable. It is obvious that Bryan was able to tap this sentiment.

However, having won, the Farrelly-Hodge administration finds itself in the coveted position of being able to derail this wave of discontent by bringing greater equity which is consonant with the American dream.

Hugo Elections in the Virgin Islands
Caribbean Contact (Barbados), February 1990: 10.

T HE NEXT GUBERNATORIAL election in the U.S. Virgin Islands held every four years, is scheduled for November 1990. And, with the turn of the year, political pundits are already beginning to speculate on this outcome. By so doing, they are, along with other factors, unavoidably examining what effects the politics of the hurricane relief of Hugo, will likely have on the political choices of the electorate.

In 1986 former Judge Alexander Farrelly and Mr. Derek Hodge, two U.S. trained lawyers, of Yale and Georgetown University respectively, were elected Governor and Lieutenant Governor of the tri-island territory. However, this triumph did not come about before they were forced by their principal opponents, pro-nationalist candidates Mr. Adelbert Bryan and Mr. Gilbert Sprauve, advocates of whatever elements of a pro-independence movement there are, into a runoff: the latter receiving 35 percent of the vote. By contrast, after taking up residence in the Governor's official residence located at Charlotte Amalie, capital of the U.S. Virgin Islands, Judge Farrelly, as head of a booming tourist economy in which "native" Virgin Islanders have little control indicated that he intended to be "the most pro-business governor in the history of the territory."

As the tenures of the Governor and Lt. Governor approach expiration, the norm in the political culture of this off-shore U.S. territory is usual for past and/or sitting senators in the 15-member elected Legislature, to form a political dyad that is sufficiently balanced in its appeal to woo the votes in both St. Thomas-St. John as well as St. Croix Districts, the last being the largest and whose voter support is indispensable for victory.

This history of the pre-election leadership strategy typically revolves around personalities and noticeably takes little consideration of party affiliation though three political parties do exist. They are the Democratic and Republican parties, replicas found on the U.S. mainland as well as the homegrown Independence Citizen Movement started by former Governor Cyril E. King.

And what of the relationship between disasters and political votes? In other words, what effect will the politics of the hurricane relief of Hugo have on the political choices of the electorate in the November election?

Before Hugo struck the U.S. Virgin Islands, the combination of Farrelly/Hodge, who had already declared their intention to stand for re-election, seemed in an upbeat mood. Their optimism stemmed from, among other things, progress on the Cyril E. King Airport project which was stalled for years and fulfillment of the promise of overdue back-pay to workers.

However, in the devastation the territory suffered, though not caused by Gov. Farrelly, he has come to be viewed as an integral part of the public management of the problems caused by Hugo and therefore accountable for their speedy amelioration.

Whether real or perceived, the slowness and unevenness in redressing many of the Hugo-related problems on the three-island territory, with St. Croix feeling very much the stepchild, is related to the predictability of political support for the incumbents. Though both are natives of St. Croix, the outcome seems less unsure for Mr. Hodge who has spent much more time there and is an active member of the Virgin Islands National Guard which is at the heart of the recovery effort.

However, Governor Farrelly hopes, in the long run, to convince the voters to return him to the office. In the coming months, he will attempt to show, with U.S. Federal Emergency Funds at his disposal, that he is capable of exceptional, effective and strong management. If this is accomplished, it will reassure his re-election with or without Mr. Hodge as a running mate, and regardless of who are his opponents.

Another viewpoint is that the hardships at the community level, particularly in St. Croix which was hard hit and whose support is key to victory, will overtake the impact of any disaster management, that can be demonstrated.

It is much too early to precisely and accurately predict the long-term effects of Hugo on the upcoming November election. However, it is safe to say that with few persons in the political arena who are seen as viable options and in the absence of the Bryan-Sprauve challenge, which has been obviously weakened by Hugo, the probability of Governor Farrelly serving a second term is not to be ruled out.

Filter the Promises and Vote Your Conscience

St Croix Avis, November 2-3, 2014: 8; VI Daily News, November 3, 2014: 10.

Politicians are supreme optimists, otherwise they would hardly get out of bed in the morning to face the harsh realities that await them in their quest to gain and/or retain political power.

It is to be imagined that these political operatives can only work in a state of false euphoria, particularly those without a record to defend.

This innate optimism, including the outlandish promises, which have no basis in fact, must be a great strength in maintaining their own morale allowing them to continue functioning long after normal people would have recoiled. This hyper-optimism gives them a resilience denied to us lesser morals.

However, the optimism of politicians can be problematic. It commonly raises false expectations which are impossible to fulfill and the end result is a disillusioned and disgruntled people; an electorate left with no faith in many of their political representatives. Political apathy and disaffection with the system are the worse-case scenarios.

Politicians get so accustomed to looking on the bright side of things that the glare apparently blinds them to the reality. Many make mountains of their achievements, often out of molehill-like items of good news.

The challengers – those politicians who are seeking to gain power for the first-time – are no better. They, too, make the absurd claim that if they get their chance all will be well. They equate the unseating of those in office, the incumbents, with the removal of the problems that exist. It sounds presumptuous and even stupid, but it is a simple fact of political life.

It is easy to lambast the ill-founded optimism of politicians and their propensity to suggest and advocate what might take the place of the unacceptable status quo. However, in circumstances where the electorate desire relief, politicians are apt to fill the breach. Hence, voters, in hopes of a better tomorrow, are caught in the cross-purposes of one another's needs, and are often gullible and easy prey to the promises of politicians, some of which they cannot deliver.

Political participation and voter behavior are vital parts of civic responsibility, and though some people exercise their franchise based on personal terms and along party lines, a sober and discerning approach to the casting of the ballot is to be engendered. Those persons who are elected to office and serve as public servants are entrusted with decision-making capabilities that are of paramount importance — that guide the course of the ship of state.

Hence, amidst the avalanche of outrageous promises and falsely elevated hopes, voters are well advised to filter the political rhetoric and vote based on a well-informed conscience.

◈

Glorious Uncertainties
until Voters Speak
VI Daily News, October 23, 1986: 16.

A<small>S AN ACADEMIC</small> who closely observes elections in most of the countries of the English-speaking Caribbean to date, I consider the outcome of the November election in the U.S. Virgin Islands not at all easy to predict.

Moreover, in the absence of many public opinion surveys, the "confidence" being exhibited by Julio Brady, Adelbert Bryan, Alexander Farrelly and Roy Schneider, the four major gubernatorial aspirants, offers no scientific guide to the outcome of what promises to be the most closely fought election since the late Cyril E. King led the Independent Citizens Movement Party to power in 1974. The high percentage of "undecided" voters does not make the prognostication any less difficult.

The pre-election day period is a time of posturing, promises and politicking. Each candidate desires victory and exudes that spirit. However, in the final analysis, the real winners or losers in the multi-party system of government are the people – those who are empowered with the vote.

The power to choose one's leaders to guide the ship of state did not always exist. This ability is a virtue and should be cherished and used wisely in the November election.

After all, as a territory of the United States, the power to elect a governor to office was first granted in 1970, Melvin Evans being the first, and it is a travesty that we are not yet able to vote for the president of the United States.

According to the ancient philosophers, democracy in its embryotic stage first came to Sparta, an ancient city-state. The demos (people) discovered that they were called upon to engage in combat in defense of their territory while the philosopher-kings and guardians lived lavishly and flagged under the heavy onslaughts of battle from the hordes of Athenians.

As a consequence, the people resolved that if they could be relied upon to protect the state in times of battle, they were capable to rule the state in peacetime.

However, as the population of the "republic" grew, pure democracy as envisaged by Rousseau receded, as it became more inconvenient and impractical a proposition.

Hence, representative democracy emerged. For if the representatives grew complacent and untrustworthy, then the people had the right to recall and choose others.

This device was employed by the philosophers of the 18th century, embraced during the Age of Reason and refined around the time of the Enlightenment to accommodate the French in the modern age.

Regardless, the quintessence of democracy remained. And so, the notion of the democracy of Pericles (considered by some to be the father of democracy) remains intact and will condition next month's election.

Curiously enough, this age-old system of government, although fascinating and captivating, points to the business of politics in a democratic-type society like ours as a tricky affair.

Candidates, beware! The vote is a sacred power in the hands of a constituent in an election. Irrespective of the money the politician spends, the handshaking and so on, it is not really an instrument of power which can easily be bought or canvassed.

Politicians speak loosely of "getting their votes." But a voter whose choice is not influenced by personality and patronage, but by virtue of the merit and ability of a candidate and his stand on the issues, has nothing to give, nor can his vote be bought.

One might seek to shape a voter's thinking and behavior in a way which favors a particular persuasion but does the average voter really have a vote to give anybody? I am yet to be persuaded this is the norm. The typical voter is much more clever than the average politician thinks.

What the voter does, after all is said and done, is to enter into the political closet alone with their conscience and their God; and there in the sweet stillness of the final power over the politicians and the politicos mark an "X" against the name of that candidate whom they think best represents their thoughts and ideas.

Many a vote is changed in those last fleeting seconds of the exercise of the voter's sovereignty. When the voters vote in secret, they envelope themselves in their sovereignty. During that moment of truth, their reign alone and they reign supreme for those few important but profound and far-reaching seconds. After the die has been cast, they surrender their powers to the representatives. This dimension of the democratic process is exciting and mysterious because of the uncertainty it engenders.

We attend the various debates, witness television appearances and form our impressions about the individual candidates. As individuals or as a collection of like-minded folk, we think we know which team or candidate will be the victor. But in reality, we shall never truly know until the end of what the end shall be. For the future is full of glorious uncertainties.

Vote your conscience. The future of the Virgin Islands depends upon it.

Some Conservative Religious Groups Are Politically Engaged

VI Daily News, August 29, 2006: 17.

C AN ONE'S LEADERSHIP in a Christian church be compromised by one's involvement in elective politics? Can a "true and committed" Christian circumvent the often messy business of politics? These are two questions that are proffered from time to time, especially when elections are imminent.

In the past, conservative, evangelical Christians, like Seventh-Day Adventists, took the position that the church and the individual Christian had a limited political role to play. Jehovah's Witnesses go so far as refusing to vote or even salute the national flag, believing that this would violate Jesus's statement that "My kingdom is not of this world." For them, the kingdom of God is eschatological (the last days, in the future) and the Christian's essential duty is to proclaim its imminence and bring people into a life-changing experience with Jesus, the King of the Kingdom. Politics is a no-no.

And so, since when have conservative, apocalyptic groups, like the Seventh-Day Adventists and others, often accused of folding their hands and waiting for Jesus to burst the skies, become interested in the politics of the world?

Theological rethinking within many conservative, evangelical Christian circles, have resulted in a shift in attitude. Many are now restorationists or theonomists who believe that it is God's purpose to have Christians enter politics to help clean it up. The present Bush administration in the United States echoes this thinking.

In recent years, Seventh-Day Adventists are now found in appointed and elected offices worldwide, including the Caribbean. Since 1993, James Carlisle, a Seventh - day Adventist has served as the governor general of Antigua and Barbuda. In Barbados, Victor Johnson, another Seventh - day Adventist, unseated Wes Hall, a cricket icon whose prowess as a West Indies fast bowler inspired the Mighty Gabby's song "Hit It" and who has now exchanged the magic of the ball for the pulpit.

The shift in thinking is predicated on a belief in a "kingdom-now" message, which essentially teaches that the light and salt of the earth concepts mean that the Christian's influence must begin with the kingdom of God in the here and now.

The kingdom of God is compared (in a parable of Jesus) to leaven and the mustard seed, which begin small but then grows. And so, while the restorationists wait for Jesus to usher in the perfect kingdom, it is believed that they and other Christians have a big part to play in "occupying 'til He comes," rather than waiting passively and doing nothing to advance the kingdom.

Then there is liberation theology, a fusion of Christian principles and political activism, often Marxist in character, associated with radical priests like Gustavo Gutierrez, a Catholic, and Ernle Gordon, an Anglican, who believe that these apocalyptic groups are just apologists for the system. However unwittingly, they are really serving the interest of the ruling class that is the oppressor.

These espouse a variety of "liberation theology" perspectives in which Jesus is seen as a revolutionary with a message that was subversive to the established order.

Out-group members have been sold a depoliticized Jesus in support of oppression. The real Jesus, they say, would actively encourage his followers to engage in direct political action to bring about structural, fundamental change – not changes within the system but a change of the system.

In the case of the U.S. Virgin Islands, many Christians are content to stay on the fringe of the political arena, only voting. However, others see themselves as possible agents of change, impacting on all aspects of V.I. life – the moral, social and political.

CARIBBEAN IMMIGRANT WINS SENATE SEAT IN ST. THOMAS

St. Croix Avis, November 15-16, 1992: VI Daily News, November 16, 1992: 14.

IT IS OF note that a Caribbean immigrant won one of the seven Senate seats in the 20th Legislature of the U.S. Virgin Islands. This feat appears to have made George Goodwin, an Antiguan who has lived in the Virgin Islands for 32 years, the first Caribbean immigrant to sit in the Senate as a representative for the St. Thomas-St. John district.

Goodwin's remarkable showing in the primary was a harbinger of things to come. He gained 2,689 votes and in doing so placed fourth in a field of eight, three of whom were seeking re-election. He actually gained more votes than two of the incumbent democratic senators.

And so, giving his stunning performance in the preliminary race, Goodwin, as it turned out, was a formidable challenger at a time when the electorate, both on the U.S. mainland and its Virgin Islands territory, was clamoring for change.

This penchant among many of the voters must have been influenced by the fact that the sitting of the incumbent 19th Legislature had been punctuated with internecine conflict and, in the eyes of many observers, at the expense of the more substantive issues like the quality of education and the state of the economy.

Goodwin ran on the slate of the Democratic Party which offered nine candidates altogether in a field of contenders from the Republican Party, the Independent Citizens Movement as well as independents. Only two were his match. He garnered 7,037 votes. The highest vote-getter being Judy Gomez with 8,966, followed by Bingley Richardson with 7,569.

The plank of Goodwin's pre-election campaign focused on the need for an improvement in the education system, unity in diversity and diversification of the economy. However, Goodwin, who worked assiduously as head of the Alien Interest Movement for over two decades, stayed clear of any mention of "*islandism*" – ethnic prejudice against non-natives – a pattern that has abated, but a memory of which obviously won him many a vote.

Notwithstanding this fact, Goodwin's victory could only be assured with wide support beyond that of Caribbean immigrants, who seemingly supported his candidacy, showing that they are no longer politically impotent. Though permanent residents, Caribbean immigrants, who often eschew "returning home", have been slow in becoming naturalized citizens in significant numbers. These were ineligible to vote for Goodwin or for any candidate of their choice.

However, though a Caribbean immigrant, Goodwin's campaign strategy of portraying himself as a leader for "all of the people" gained him a cross-section of voters and allowed him to clinch victory. It may well be that the election of a non-native from the Caribbean to the Virgin Islands Legislature, in the past called "*aliens*," "*down islanders*" and even "*garrots*," derogatory terms that are slowing falling into public disuse, points to an attenuation of insular politics, which tend to characterize island-societies and a maturing of the body politic.

Goodwin's victory has altered the political landscape in the Virgin Islands in that Caribbean immigrants, though their voting numbers have increased, and their contributions in such areas as religion and business are undisputable, have until this historic outcome, remained outside the halls of formal political power on St. Thomas and for that matter in the U.S. Virgin Islands.

Other ethnic groups on St. Thomas, namely the East Indians, Jews, Arabs and Asians, all wheel remarkable influence in relation to their size. By contrast, newcomers, including those who hail from the Dominican Republic and Haiti, whose votes like those of the Caribbean immigrants of yesteryear, were not vigorously wooed, are marginal and presently part of the largely politically invisible. Unlike St. Croix, Hispanics on St. Thomas are more diffuse.

The U.S. Virgin Islands is a multi-ethnic society. And so, in the context of a Legislature where white Americans, called "continentals," African-Americans, local whites known as *"Frenchies,"* Afro-Virgin Islanders, as well as women as a minority group, are represented, Caribbean immigrants on St. Thomas, who number approximately 14,204, seemed to have "come in from the cold" to claim some measure of the political empowerment which had previously eluded them.

Goodwin's bid, his second attempt to gain a Senate seat, which has now resulted in electoral success, can be construed as not merely a personal triumph for him and his coterie, but a symbolic victory for all Caribbean immigrants.

Also, in practical terms, Goodwin's triumph has the makings of contributing to improved societal cohesion in so far as his Senate seat, in potential terms, gives a political voice to a highly visible grouping who, some contend have far too long felt alienated in their adopted home.

The Cuban Card in USVI
and Caribbean Politics
St. Croix Avis, August 23, 1995: 9 & 39.

S INCE HIS ELECTION in November 1994, Gov. Roy Schneider has, on a range of issues, repeatedly shown what was already known, namely, that he is a strong leader and one who is able to implement decisions that he believes are morally right though unpopular. Most, if not all of these, an example of which is the restructuring of the top-heavy Department of Education, are on the domestic front.

However, if The VI Daily News article of Aug. 17, which states that "Washington has advised Puerto Rico and the U.S. Virgin Islands not to take up associate membership in the Association of Caribbean States" is correct, Gov. Schneider may be facing his first test, if construed as such, relative to external matters, on the territory's official attitude toward Cuba.

The outcome of this dilemma is also a measure of whether the "change is coming" theme can and does go beyond our shores and is different from the policy of his predecessor, Gov. Alexander Farrelly. Under Farrelly's charge, the U.S. V.I. gained observer status with the rest of the Caribbean in 1991, but his administration did not support Cuba's application for membership in the 24-member Caribbean Tourism Organization which subsequently became a reality.

On Dec. 8, 1972, Jamaica under Michael Manley, Trinidad and Tobago under Eric Williams, Barbados under Errol Barrow and Guyana under Forbes Burnham, in defiance of the U.S. diplomatic, trade and economic embargo against Cuba, jointly established diplomatic relations with that country. Three of these prime ministers died in office in the 1980s and with them an era of strong leadership. Manley, who resigned from active politics in 1991, is still a defender of the "politics of Castroism."

U.S. military action on the Spice Island of Grenada, in cooperation with some Caribbean states, in October 1983, in the wake of the bloody coup against the People's Revolutionary Government, Prime Minister Maurice Bishop among its slain victims, seriously rupturing Cuban-Caricom relations.

However, in contrast to the past, the decade of the 90s started with deepened cooperation among Cuba and Caricom countries with the reopening of a Cuban diplomatic mission in Jamaica in 1991. Diplomatic ties with Havana were broken off in 1982 in the wake of the Grenada crisis. The "Iron Lady of the Caribbean," Dominica's Eugenia Charles, who on account of her pro-U.S. stance received the first James Monroe Memorial Award from President Reagan at a U.S. State Department dinner, had before demitting office, come around to encouraging trade with Cuba. Even Grenada has normalized its relations with Cuba after nine years of tension.

While the U.S. has little flinched on its 21-year trade, economic and financial embargo against Cuba, Caricom nations in 1992 overwhelmingly supported an approved United Nations General Assembly resolution calling for a termination of that embargo. There were three votes against: U.S., Israel and Romania.

In 1993, two major developments deepened Cuba-Caricom relations. First, Cuba's 39-year old Foreign Minister Roberto Robaima Gonzalez, the youngest member of President Castro's cabinet, paid a seven-nation official visit to the region. Robaima's delegation included Cuba's ambassador to Barbados, other Eastern Caribbean countries and the

Bahamas. Second, the Caricom Joint Commission was established on the heels of this visit with a group of U.S. congressmen, including Robert G. Torrecelli of New Jersey, threatening that this could result in the loss of potential benefits from the U.S.

And so, at a time when many of the political leaders in the neighboring Caribbean as well as such countries as Canada, India, Australia, France, Spain and Sweden are lending increasing support to Cuba because they believe it to be the morally right thing to do, it will be interesting to see how Gov. Schneider's strong leadership will play the Cuban card. Will he take the course of least resistance and do the politically expedient thing —heed the advice of Washington and not take up membership of the Association of Caribbean States which recently completed its inaugural summit in Trinidad, an event attended by 25 Caribbean and Latin American leaders, including those from dependent territories, or will his decision to join the ACS point to what is regarded in some quarters as the consistency in his strong leadership of and for the territory?

If the latter course of action prevails, it would be tantamount, in political terms, to "David showing Goliath" that, in the post-cold war period, rapprochement with Cuba is the more prudent option.

Voting: A Right and a Responsibility

VI Daily News, October 31, 2018: 22.

T HE RIGHT TO vote is precious beyond words. On November 6, 2018, after the early voting possibilities, those registered and eligible to vote can venture to the polls and have the benefit of the opportunity to help elect the next Government of the US Virgin Islands.

The next set of key officials is three-tiered: 15 senators who make up the unicameral Legislature; a delegate to Congress and a governor/ lieutenant team - the head of the executive branch - which is obviously the weightiest. The members of the third branch of government, the judges that make up the judiciary, are appointed.

The freedom to elect or re-elect public servants to office for fixed periods of time, two years for senators; two years for the delegate to Congress and four years for the governor and his or her running-mate, is both a right and a responsibility.

Prior to 1937, the right to vote was restricted. No resident of the territory, namely St. Croix, St. Thomas, St. John and Water Island could exercise the franchise. The U.S. Congress' passage of the Organic Act brought the greatest amount of self-government the islands had ever known. For the first time, all islanders 21 years of age and older enjoyed universal suffrage.

For the governor, that right was extended to every adult in 1970. Melvin Evans was the last to be appointed and the first to be elected. With this, full representative government, a modicum of democracy, at last came to American's Paradise. Previously, governors were appointed by the President of the United States.

Yet we sometimes treat this precious right to vote as a matter of little importance, even though the ancestors fought for it tenaciously. Activists including David Hamilton Jackson and Rothschild Francis laid the foundation. Therefore, it ill becomes us to treat the right to vote with indifference or as something of little value.

It is a right from which we should not absolve ourselves, except in the case of overriding religious reasons. (Jehovah's Witnesses and some strands of Rastafari refrain from participating in the political process).

After a good showing, Angel Dawson, who served as Finance Commissioner in the John deJongh Administration, with former Staff Judge Advocate of the VI National Guard, Marise James, as his running mate as well as Allison "Allie" Petrus, who served 3 terms in the legislature and Samuel Sanes, a sitting senator, were both eliminated in a keenly-contested Democratic Primary. These two embattled teams have since thrown their support behind the winner, Bryan and Roach with the theme "Voters say *change course now*." Albert Bryan Jr., is a former VI Labor commissioner in the deJongh administration and Tregenza Roach, a senator in the 30th, 31st and 32nd Legislatures.

As so, the incumbents Governor Kenneth Mapp-Lt. Governor Osbert Potter's bid for a second term is being challenged, not only by the Bryan-Roach dyad but 5 others, including some odd couples, who hope to succeed them. These are Moleto Smith Jr. and his running-mate Lorenzo Frederick; Janette Millin Young a four-term Democratic senator, running as an independent, with Edgar Bengoa; Soraya Diase Coffelt, a defiant and short-lived Attorney General for the Mapp administration with Dwight Nicholson and Alicia "Chucky" Hansen, an 11-term senator, has joined with Adlah Donastorg Jr., who served 7 terms in the VI legislature beginning in 1996. Finally, Warren Mosler, a self-styled economist and one-time sports car engineer, who once ran for lieutenant-governor with Diase Coffelt, has teamed up with Ray Fonseca, "a bit of a political unknown."

These offerings, each with a running-mate on the sister-island of St. Croix, show an exodus of 4 senators not seeking reelection and who now aspire for greener pastures. That number could have been 5. Sitting Senator Positive Nelson, chose a St. Thomas businessman, Gary Udhwani, as his running mate, but later dropped out of the governor's race.

Voting is a right for which people have died. It is a right greatly to be treasured. It is a responsibility that no one else can shoulder for us.

Thus far in the election year, to the credit of the candidates, the political campaigning has been largely free of personal vilification and character assassinations. In addition, there has been no scientific polling of people's opinions telling us the likelihood of a candidate or team being voted into or out of office. Anecdotal accounts are inconclusive.

For voters who are strong, die-hard supporters of a candidate or team, the choice is predictable and easy. Sentiments amount to unqualified support: "*Da is ma cousin and ma friend*." For voters not so strongly attached to the candidate or political party, other factors and a more rational and matter-of-fact calculations are likely to influence their choice. They may consider the relative merits of the candidates such as his or her demonstrable leadership skills.

They may consider how the incumbent government performed, pre-and post-Hurricanes Irma, and Maria in 2017, with particular reference to the economic management of tourism the linchpin of the economy, and the needs of VI farmers. Have they extended welfare services, including to the elderly, mentally ill and the homeless as well as the delivery of health care services to obviate out-of-territory travel to receive care.

Choices this time around may be affected by even more concerns, including the Water and Power Authority and its power outages and soaring utility bills; retroactive payments for teachers and GERS with its failing retirement system and all that implies. Even the increasing arrogant behavior or theatrics of the incumbents could strongly affect voters' choices.

A poignant question for some voters could very well be whether incumbents, warts and all, should be reelected, considering the cynical saying "It is better to love the devil/angel you know than the one you don't know."

Some would-be voters have become increasingly fed up with the system and are not excited about either of the candidates, parties or teams because the political elite, present and prospective, rightly or wrongly, is seen as taking turns in mismanaging the economy, including the territory's financial resources.

Humans are admittedly sentimental, but voting is so important that the choices should be made only after very careful consideration and thought. Voter behavior is the only means residents of the territory have to determine who will be the ones to govern.

If we are not comfortable with any the candidates, the least we can do is - by the process of elimination - vote for the ones we consider 'the lesser of the evils.' But by all means vote!

IV

THE MILITARY OF BARBADOS

Tom Adams: Architect of the Eastern Caribbean Military Build-up

Barbados Advocate December 26, 1987: 7.

T HANKS FOR THE opportunity to respond to a <u>Barbados Advocate</u> newspaper editorial, January 26, 1987, entitled, "The Question of Militarization" in which I was accused of two pronouncements relative to the emphasis on the military in Barbados while Prime Minister Tom Adams and the Barbados Labor Party were in power. Both allegations stem from two of my published articles on the subject. One entitled "Caribbean Militarization: A Response to Crisis," <u>Contemporary Marxism,</u> vol. 10, 1985: 92-109, and the other "Barbados and the Militarization of the Eastern Caribbean, 1979-85", in the <u>Bulletin of Eastern Caribbean Affairs</u>, vol. 11, 6, 1986: 8-18.

The editorial in question which, I have confirmed was written by historian F.A. Hoyas, flatly deny that Adams was the architect behind the military build-up in the Eastern Caribbean sub-region in the 1980's. Secondly, it accuses me of definitively and conclusively establishing a positive causal relationship between Adams being an avid reader of war-related material, a readily known fact, and his role as the mastermind behind the military build-up.

Here is the true story. As part of my ongoing research on the military in the Commonwealth Caribbean and, in particular, my preparation for a paper on the military and security in the Caribbean at the

Caribbean Studies Association Conference, Belize, May 26, 1987, I wrote Adamsonian historian, Sir F.A. Hoyas, putting the proposition of Adams's known predilection for reading war-related materials and his military posture before the good gentleman. I was simply exploring, inquiring and soliciting his impressions and sentiments on an issue that any thinking person and serious-minded scholar interested in matters of this sort would regard as plausible. I was not categorical in any way. The inquiry was made by letter (December 15, 1986) and Hoyas' return letter was dated January 24, 1987.

In regards to my aforementioned article, at no point in the narratives do I state or imply any such assertion. As it turned out, Hoyas chose to jump the gun and engage in the untruth that I had published in the <u>Bulletin of Eastern Caribbean Affairs</u> that I had arrived at the stated conclusion. This is just not so, and the article speaks for itself. However, even though I will not advise that psychological reductionism be employed as a sufficient means to adequately understand Barbados military policy, I do believe that the hypothesized relationship between Adams's great interest in military history and his status as a quasi-military oriented figure is plausible; deserves further study and should not be ignored. The known personality traits of major political leaders and the advocacy and shaping of policy should not be easily dismissed.

Secondly, in regards to Hoyos's refutation that Adams is not the architect of the Eastern Caribbean military build-up, I have quarrel, in this instance, with his method of research and his calculus for arriving at social facts. He states that Professor Phillips' claim is unsound and unbalanced because he has "not read the speeches by Mr. Louis Tull and Senator John Wickham in the House of Assembly on the occasion of Adams' death" and that if I, Professor Phillips, were to do so, I would put the matter "in the right perspective."

Come on, Mr. Hoyas, you know full well that utterances made on or around the occasion of a person's death and during the period of mourning, as was the case, are typically magnanimous and given to fawning and must be weighed in that context.

The historian and scientist, in his/her pursuit of an understanding of social reality/political culture ought not ignore or behave as though such outpourings were never made. However, any such statements must necessarily be checked against the larger picture. I am acquainted with those distinguished speeches delivered, by the way, by two of Adams's staunch supporters, including Mr. Louis Tull serving as his Minister of External Affairs, and am still of the mind that Adams was the architect behind the military build-up. The unprecedented increase in the share of governmental expenditure allocated to military purposes in Barbados under Adams' tenure, as well as his role in the creation of the Regional Security System belie Hoyos's counterclaim that Adams was not the military master-mind that I purport him to be. The Adams doctrine of electing to win "in the field" through troop deployment rather than through negotiations is evidenced in Union Island and Grenada, and buttresses the argument that Adams attached undue importance to defense. Adams likely regarded the display and use of the "military and security arms of the state" as an added symbol of sovereignty and was manifestly prepared to serve in a kind of sub-imperialist role. Indeed, the notion has been advanced that Adams's presentation of his political self in the arena of politics gave credence to the notion that he may have believed in the dictum that it is really better for the Prince to be feared than loved.

In his denial of Adams' role as the architect, Hoyas used the non-sequitur that Adams's purpose was "to preserve the cause of parliamentary democracy in Grenada and the other territories of the Caribbean." Well yes, by Hoyos's own show of interest; his need to preserve the superficial and limited image of Adams and contain the revisionist view of Adams as the junior partner in the militarization of Barbados and the Eastern Caribbean, tells the tale.

If, at all, a solid argument can be mounted to debunk the characterization of Prime Minister Tom Adams as the man behind the military build-up in Barbados and the Eastern Caribbean in the 1980's, Hoyos's efforts to do so are transparently feeble and unconvincing. Come again, Mr. Hoyos.

❖

Put Opposition on Defense Force Board

Daily Nation (Barbados), June 11. 1987: 7.

I N October 1983, while Prime Minister Tom Adams and the Barbados Labor Party (BLP) were the duly elected Government of Barbados, the unsettling events in Grenada led to the deployment to that country, of a detachment of the Barbados Defense Force (BDF) in support of the 82nd Airborne Division of the U.S. military establishment. The BLP, as it did then, continues to stoutly defend its action, whereas the ranks of the Democratic Labor Party (DLP) seems to exhibit a certain ambivalence. The very able Cameron Tudor stated that the U.S. Naval Facility in St. Lucy should never have left Barbados, whereas, P.M. Barrow openly denounced U.S. action.

October this year will be four years since that historic event occurred. It is felt by some that the matter is a fait accompli and should be laid to rest. However, Sir Cameron Tudor's recent statements, relative to crisis management involving the use of the BDF, is cause for pause and raises a more fundamental and far reaching question regarding future use of the BDF.

Part II, Section 1, p. 14 of the <u>Barbados Defense Force Act 1979</u> states that the Barbados Defense Board, of whom the Prime Minister and the BDF Chief of Staff are key members, is responsible for the command of the defense force and, I presume that to mean, its operational use.

Notably, the Act makes no provision for representation of the opposition on said Board. I have not examined other Commonwealth Defense Force Acts and am, therefore, not sure this will constitute a precedent. However, I suggest that an amendment to the Barbados Defense Force Act of 1979 be considered to permit the inclusion of members of the opposition, perhaps two. Such an accommodation will not hinder the taking of prompt and effective security matters, nor will it detract from the doctrine of government responsibility. Rather, it would encourage, not prevent, consultation between the government of the day and the opposition on matters of foreign military policy and, by so doing, better ensure the proper use of the BDF.

Defense Force Needs Good Public Relations

Daily Nation (Barbados), June 3, 1995: 6.

ONE AREA IN the growth and development of the Barbados Defense Force (BDF) that appears to lag behind its many accomplishments is the need for improved public relations.

Though it can be argued that the basis of good public relations is good behavior, the latter, though necessary, is not sufficient. In the case of the BDF, there is still room for better mutual understanding between this institution and the public.

This reality can come about with the appointment of a public relations officer to serve as a liaison officer between the BDF and the public, as is presently the case with the Royal Barbados Defense Force.

This recommendation is not based on a need to extract classified and confidential information. In its own interest, the BDF must make it possible for the public to better understand the purpose, needs, accomplishments and aspirations of this institution.

The best way to prevent rumors, leaks and half-truths in a disciplined organization is not to muzzle officers and other ranks, but to get the relevant facts to the public and not rationalize unwarranted secrecy on the "no need to know" principle.

The BDF must anticipate the need to provide explanations of unpopular measures that it may have to take in the future. The adoption of this suggested policy position is the more compelling in view of the fact that the BDF will, more than likely, be called upon in the future to again perform peacekeeping duties in conflicts outside of Barbados and in some instances under the umbrella of the United Nations.

V

RELIGION AND THEOLOGY

◆

BETTER TO GIVE THAN RECEIVE, CHRISTMAS OR NO CHRISTMAS

VI Daily News, January 2, 1986:14.

1985 IS RACING to an end. Another Christmas has just been celebrated. And, of course, this time of the year is associated with gift-giving, if nothing more than a card.

Those among us who grew up in small, close-knit communities like Savan, St. Thomas; Sandy Point, St. Kitts, or a small sleepy hamlet in upstate New York will remember the perennial community spirit which abounded. Giving was important and much practiced. People gave freely of their goods, their time and their talents, not only at Christmas, but all year round.

No more, sad to say; nowadays, such behavior hardly characterizes late 20th century society, whether it be in the Caribbean or elsewhere.

In contemporary times, with the coming of "progress" and as urbanization sprawls into areas like TuTu, still ironically designated "country," the economic changes have brought profound transformation in the Virgin Islander's social life.

These days spontaneous giving has, in far too many instances, given way to the "quid pro quo" – something for something, and in some instances, something for nothing.

Why is this? A frequently heard explanation is that because of the unprecedented cost of living, economic deprivation is much more acute. People are still inclined to give, it is said, but they cannot afford the luxury of giving. Harsh economic realities make giving prohibitive.

This, however, is false. Economic deprivation in bygone days was by no means any less austere than today; giving was not a luxury item. The marked difference was that in those days, it was a joy to give. It seems as though there was a greater appreciation for the principle that everyone was his/her "brother's keeper." It is that simple.

Another explanation is that the many pressures of our modern, complex society have made people selfish, cold and uncaring. But were there not many exigencies in those far off days like the devastating infant mortality rate, disease and poverty?

But somehow, in spite of these debilitating social and economic conditions, people found time and saw the need to be generous and concerned.

With the advent of progress, development or whatever analytical construct you may care to employ, seemingly, people are typically better equipped to give. However, the converse is the case.

Individualism and materialism have become more flagrant, widespread and even acceptable. People delight in selfishly doing their own thing and, will remind you of their right to do so.

These days, even the fundamentalist "other-world or oriented" churches, whose proud refrain is that "this world is not my home," have begun to succumb to the "me-for-me" syndrome.

The Pentecostals, Seventh-day Adventists and a few others are probably the last bastions of relative selflessness. Even for these groupings, there are already signs of capitulation to more secular mores.

The whole pattern of life has been altered. Family structure, which according to some social commentators is the heart of the social fabric of any society, has undergone drastic change. The extended family has been dismantled and is being replaced by the nuclear family. The recent census figures point to the astronomical increase in single-parent families.

And so, with the coming of modernization in the Virgin Islands beginning in the 1950s, our society's institutions have changed and so have the personalities of those who live here. This is evidenced in the manifest erosion of a once-held willingness to give.

But must the passing of an era be looked upon as an artifact of the past and nothing more? Can we not attempt to salvage some of the worthwhile and desirable features from the wreckage of past times?

Do we acquiesce to the popular notion that it is more blessed to give than to receive only if we're boxers in a ring? Or do we seek to understand afresh the teachings of the synoptic gospels of Mark and Luke?

Perhaps, we do well to reflect upon the words of Kahlil Gibran, the Lebanese poet and philosopher in the "The Prophet":

> There are those who give little
> of the much which they have – and
> they give it for recognition and
> their hidden desires make their
> gifts unwholesome. And there are
> those who have little and give it all.
> These are the believers in life and
> the bounty of life, and their coffer
> is never empty.

Fair ye well and remember that it is often times better to give than to receive, Christmas or no Christmas.

Televangelists are Hustlers Masquerading as God's Men

VI Daily News, August 13, 1987: 6.

T HESE DAYS, THERE is much talk about so called "holy war" among Pentecostals in the electronic church. It was sparked off by the revelation of Jim Baker's dalliance with Jessica Hahn from Long Island, N. Y.

Jim and his wife, Tammy, who catered to the religious needs of millions of their supporters in the United States and around the world, have not only fallen from grace, but they have, almost overnight, lost control of their religious empire, Heritage USA, and other assets.

The loss is much greater. Because of Baker's visibility as a preacher and host of the PTL or Praise the Lord TV Club, his action, which recently came to light after seven years of cover, has, in its aftermath, like a vortex, cast a dark shadow over Christians everywhere.

It has served to taint fellow TV evangelists Jimmy Swaggart, Robert Schuller, and others. Pioneer media and globetrotting evangelist Billy Graham seems to be above the fray.

Such non-exemplary behavior among Christians, especially from the leadership, looms large and is cause for concern. However, turmoil has punctuated the history of the church, and this recent episode will not be the last.

The heritage of religion is one of war. From the inception, war broke out in the city of God. Lucifer was hurdled from heaven for his rebellion against the government of God.

That "original sin" led to the contamination of Adam and Eve, and man and woman have been falling ever since. Jim Baker just happens to be the most recent and celebrated case.

There was trouble in the "early church" during the days of the Apostle Paul, as well as of Peter, referred to in some quarters as the first pope. We know about the famous row when King Henry VIII of England broke away from the authority of the pope and the Catholic Church. The pope balked at Henry's request for a divorce, and Henry retaliated by getting rid of Cardinal Thomas Wolsey and forming what is today called Anglicanism or Episcopalianism.

Martin Luther broke away from the Catholic Church in Germany because, in his view, the pope and the church were corrupt. That schism resulted in the creation of the Lutheran Church, among others.

We are cautioned against being smug or casting stones at anyone. Closer to home, infighting within the Virgin Islands Episcopalian Church over the selection of a bishop has simmered with the appointment of E. Ron Taylor, a talented Jamaican, to that vital post.

Also, the appointment of G. Ralph Thompson, a Black Barbadian as the No. 2 man in the world Church or General Conference of the Seventh-Day Adventists has attenuated the clamoring for black unions and somewhat eased the racial climate among the brethren on the mainland.

Both in the historical and contemporary churches, there was and is ample evidence of sustained interpersonal conflict, theological revisionism and schism among professed Christians.

Man that is born of a woman is by definition, weak. The clergy and other exemplars of that genre are no exceptions. It is only the grace of

God that is capable of redeeming man. Far too often, the "true believers" put preachers on too high a pedestal and above scrutiny.

Caribbean people must be vigilant. The evidence is mounting that many, if not all, of the leading TV evangelists are hustlers who masquerade as "men of God." Religion is just another commodity to be packaged and sold with all the trappings.

Without infringing on First Amendment rights, a mechanism needs to be put in place to exact more accountability, so that these charlatans will desist from preying on their followers, the vast majority of whom are simple folk who regard religion as a way to cope and imbue their lives with meaning. The same mechanism should protect the integrity of Christian believers everywhere.

Consumers of religion must focus on "the message" and not the messenger. Man, the medium, is weak and often the preachers are enmeshed by the bureaucracy that seeks to bring out the worst in earthlings with good intentions who are supposedly called by God to lead the flock.

Recent events in the religious community have divided, not united, the body of Christ. Now is the time for reconciliation. The wounds will heal, but the scars of this religious conflict will very likely never be erased.

One thing is sure. The word of God will endure forever, no matter how weak the human vessel that espouses it. Preachers are no worse than politicians. God is in heaven; with Him, and in Him, there is peace, not war.

Pope Francis, Cuba and Christian Unity

VI Daily News, March 5, 2016: 22 and 24.

Pope Francis's meeting in Cuba on Feb. 12, 2016, with the head of the Russian Orthodox Church, Patriarch Krill of Moscow, is a signal that this pontiff, the first Jesuit to hold this position, is a trendsetter and a crusader for the restoration of unity among Christians. He seemed destined to play a strategic and prophetic role in shaping Christianity and the future of the world, perceived by some evangelicals and others as part of the unfolding of "last day events."

During the first few centuries, politically significant cities like Rome, Alexandria, Antioch and Constantinople each had their own bishop. By the 11ᵗʰ century, the bishop of Rome had started to claim prominence. In fact, the western branch of the church believed that the bishop of Rome was the successor to St. Peter, one of Jesus' disciples, who had been martyred in Rome. As such, the Rome bishop was thought to have authority over the other bishops.

This posture by Rome coupled with other theological and political differences resulted in the schism of AD 1054, which ultimately led to the division of the Eastern Christian churches and the Western Church, popularly known as the Roman Catholic Church.

Today, both branches of the church – the Roman Catholic Church and Eastern Orthodoxy – claim apostolic succession – they trace their history to an unbroken line straight to Jesus and his Twelve. As a result, both assert that they are the one, true original church founded by Jesus during his time on earth. Also, a number of other doctrinal differences still exist, including whether priests can be married and the very nature of the Trinity.

There are about 260 million Orthodox Christians compared to 1.2 billion Roman Catholics around the world. While Roman Catholics still consider the pope to be their spiritual leader, Eastern Orthodoxy is organized like a federation of 15 local churches of ethnic origins (like the Greek Orthodox Church, the Romanian Orthodox Church and the Russian Orthodox Church). Each of these churches has its own head or patriarch and is led by the ecumenical patriarch of Constantinople, Bartholomew 1, in Turkey who considers himself to be the first among equals, though he doesn't officially hold any special authority over the other patriarchs.

Attempts at reconciliation between the Roman Catholic Church and the Eastern Orthodoxy have been made throughout the centuries (some as early as 1274) and there has been progress in recent years. Pope John Paul VI met with the ecumenical patriarch in Constantinople back in 1964. Francis has done the same during his time at the Vatican.

Both of Francis's two predecessors, John Paul II and Benedict XVI, tried but failed to reach agreement to hold talks with the head of the Russian Orthodox Church, with the prospect of a wider and eventual Christian unity.

The significance of Pope Francis' recent meeting with the head of the Russian Orthodox Church lies in the fact that the Russian Orthodox Church counts 165 million of the world's 250 million orthodox Christians. It is not only the largest but also wealthiest and most powerful branch of Eastern Orthodoxy. Also, Patriarch Krill, its leader, has pursued closer ties with Russian President Vladimir Putin and the Kremlin.

And so, what are the apparent backward and forward politico-religious linkages between Pope Francis, Patriarch Krill; the Castro brothers and the site of the rendezvous. Back in 20 October 2008, while on a tour of Latin America, Fidel Castro commended Metropolitan Krill as his ally in combatting "American Imperialism." Krill later rewarded Raul Castro and Fidel Castro, who has since ceded power to his brother, the order of St. Daniel of Moscow, on the behalf of Patriarch Alexy II in recognition of their decision to build the first Russian Orthodox Church in Havana, to serve Russian expatriates living there.

On arrival in Castro's Cuba, the two religious leaders, Pope Francis and Patriarch Krill, kissed each other three times on the cheek at the Jose Marti International Airport in Havana. "Finally!" Francis exclaimed as they embraced. "We are brothers." Krill told the pope through an interpreter. "Now things are easier." Krill had previously stated that there could be no doctrinal compromise with the Roman Catholic Church and that discussions with them did not have the goal of unification. Notwithstanding, he has been criticized by the conservative wing of the Russian Orthodox Church for practicing ecumenism and associating himself with the Catholic Church.

No wonder that the path breaking meeting, the first time that the leader of the Roman Catholic Church met with the head of the Russian Orthodox Church, was brokered by Cuban President Raul Castro, who hosted the pope in Cuba last year and is a possible payback for the Vatican's role in the normalization of relations with Cuba and the United States, after diplomatic relations were severed in 1961.

In spite of their differences and the misgivings in the Russian Orthodox Church, Pope Francis and Russian Krill's private meeting lasted for three hours. Afterwards, they signed a 30-point joint declaration, prepared in advance, addressing global issues. These include the persecution of Christians by militants in the Middle East, Africa and other regions of the world, calling on political leaders to take action; the need for joint counter-measures for the defense of their conservative doctrine and values, including the traditional family, against the rising tide of secularism as well as their hope for the re-establishment of full Christian unity.

By hosting the unprecedented meeting between Pope Francis and Patriarch Krill, Cuba, a Caribbean country, continues to play a big role in shaping not only the political but religious landscape in global affairs. Barack Obama's scheduled visit to Cuba next month will be the first by a sitting US president in over 50 years.

Being an ocean away from Europe where both churches – the Eastern and Western – have had territorial disputes in the past and given Cuba's historical ties to Russia during the Cold War, the Francis-Krill rendezvous in Cuba, now a fait accompli, was a huge meeting arranged by and on a small island. It could prove to be a turning point toward the coming unification of Christianity as Rome solidifies its church-state alliances and attempted to further centralize its religious power. If not more, the encounter between Pope Francis and Patriarch Krill of the Russian Orthodox Church was a symbolic step toward a nearly 1,000-year-old schism within Christianity. And though the full effects that this meeting will have on Christian unity remains to be seen, it is very likely to be a harbinger of things to come and one of the coming waves of the future. The last moments will be rapid ones.

Pope Francis: Change without Change

VI Daily News, November 28, 2015: 26-27.

From the very start, Jorge Mario Bergoglio's expected election in 2013 and subsequent installation as the 266th Supreme Pontiff has been punctuated with surprises. He is continually breaking new ground. He is the first pope from the Southern Hemisphere. He is the first Jesuit pope, even though the Society of Jesus tends to discourage its members from holding high office. He is the first pope to take the moniker Francis, after Francis of Assisi, patron of the poor. There have been 14 Clements, 16 Benedicts and 21 Johns, but never a Francis.

The firsts continue. He is the first pope to address a joint session of the U.S. Congress. Not only is his recent visit to Cuba a first for him, but also he is the first pontiff to have two bishops from two small, developing nations in the Caribbean – Haiti's Chibly Langlois and Dominica's Kelvin Felix – among his list of more than 120 cardinals worldwide. This shows the widening and deepening of the ties that bind Rome to the satellite Catholic churches in the world, especially the Caribbean.

Bergoglio – born in Buenos Aires, Argentina – was apparently elected in large part because the Vatican needed an outsider. He was hardly expected to be an iconoclast but the hope was that he could reform the Curia, the Catholic Church's bureaucratic machine in Rome – that he would address and redress some of the "shake your head" issues that affect all faith communities.

It is proffered in some quarters that the current Curia's dysfunctions were not given adequate attention by his immediate predecessors, the charismatic and globetrotting John Paul II, and Benedict XVI, the scholar and emeritus pope. These include the laxity in dealing with clergy who abuse children. They further include efforts to remove priests who engage in grave and scandalous acts, attempts often stymied by church law. A tough zero-tolerance approach globally seems to be needed, similar to the one developed in 2002 after the abuse scandal erupted in the U.S., to protect children from clergy who are pedophiles and pederasts.

In an attempt to fill the breach, Pope Francis established and chairs an eight-cardinal advisory council that ostensibly operates independently of the existing bureaucracy. The touchstone is to "reflect on the orientations and proposals for the reform of the Roma Curia," reshape the identity of Roman Catholicism, and respond to the challenges facing the church in a changing world.

However, Bergoglio's election, attractive as it was to the electorate, and his 2015 visit to the United States, widely acclaimed as it was, do not dispel an underlying current of unease among his cardinals and others. His spontaneity and unscripted outpourings have given some Catholics cause for pause and caught others off-guard.

Nine years ago in Buenos Aires, while an archbishop, Bergoglio knelt on a stage with evangelicals at an ecumenical event and asked them to pray for him. The image of him kneeling with clergy of supposedly lower rank disturbed many Roman Catholics and led to a front-page article branding him an apostate. However, some considered this encounter a deft and tactical gesture since all other make-shift faiths are welcome to take the journey home to the "fullness of truth" in keeping with authentic apostolic succession. Those other faiths, jaded by the history, theology and perceived "prophetic role" of the Catholic Church, kept distance.

Regarding women who consider abortion because of poverty and rape, Pope Francis asked: "Who can remain unmoved before such painful situations?" His now famous 'who am I to judge' retort to a query about homosexuality was also interpreted by left-leaning Catholics as a softening of the church's position and have led some elements in the media to describe Francis as "evolving" on abortion, homosexuality and marriage. Nothing could be further from the truth.

As it turns out, Catholics are far right of many of the other established churches, such as Episcopalians and Lutherans. They refuse to change the traditional stance of the church banning female priests, and continue to uphold the mandatory celibacy of the clergy. In certain circumstances, some married men who are priests from other faiths have been allowed to convert to Roman Catholicism, and some widowers with families have become priests later. However, Roman Catholic tradition does not allow men who have already "married the church" to later marry a wife.

In passing, Evangelical Protestants, like Seventh-day Adventists and other fundamentalists, who eschew an overly secular vision of morality, tend to align with Catholics on many of the cultural wars, including the right to life, traditional marriage, human sexuality, and men-only as priests. These absolutes are non-negotiable and not unique to Pope Francis and Roman Catholicism.

Though Pope Francis has said that the future of the Church requires a more active role for women, he has rejected the idea of ordaining them. Also, the ban of contraceptives, a policy that some argue places women at risk, has gone untouched, though said to be under review. Transubstantiation which holds that the bread and wine are the actual body and blood of Christ, is sacrosanct and untouchable.

And so, Pope Francis's bold stand-alone inclusive statements, though resulting in rising expectations, are hard to find in the official Catholic statements of belief and practice. His pronouncements, which have earned him the label of a reformer, appear to be attempts to forge a new social configuration which may result at best in minimalist adjustments and adaptations within the existing protocols of the Catholic Church.

Notwithstanding, the new pontiff will very likely walk in the footsteps of his predecessor's conservative theology.

Francis may well use his papacy, which began in March 2013, to root out corruption, careerism and other problems in the Curia. However, in the Catholic theology landscape, many of his statement raise false hopes in an arena in which change is less likely to occur. Dogma cannot change, though traditions can.

The fundamental beliefs or doctrines of most Protestant churches (some 45,000 currently in the world) are not etched in stone. Further development of truths and teaching could be added. However, the Catechism of the Catholic Church, along with its sacraments, beliefs and practices, are nearly immutable; tend toward continuity and may not be susceptible to further development. They are not part of the moral and malleable machinery of society.

If this be the case, the pithy statements of Pope Francis that endear him to others and portend change and inclusivism are more pastoral than doctrinal in nature. Pope Francis may have brought a humble, non-judgmental, compassionate approach to his office and hence may be ready to change select cultural traits, for example, the granting of absolution to women who have had an abortion as well as simplifying the process of marriage annulments. He has, however, not changed Catholic dogma that holds that homosexual activity, extramarital sex and abortions are sinful; do not have a place in the Catholic worldview and he will firmly adhere to the sola scriptura principle and the fundamental traditions of his church. For Roman Catholicism and Pope Francis, the more things change, the more they remain the same.

Seeing Islam through Christian Eyes

VI Daily News, March 11, 2017: 22 and 25.

For many Christians, the Quran is a forbidden book. However, Christians should understand Muslims. If they want Muslims to respect them – which means knowing about their traditions and practices – then Christians owe Muslims the same courtesy. This means not only knowing what is in the Quran but how Muslims have interpreted that text over time.

Islam, with approximately 1.3 billion followers worldwide, is second to Christianity among the world's religions.

Although news and events and a worldview of Orientalism suggest an inherent conflict with Christians and Muslims, the two faiths, though different, are similar in many ways and share points of convergence.

Both are monotheistic and believe in a single God, as opposed to atheists or polytheists. Christians and Muslims do share the belief in the miraculous birth of Jesus, though Muslims do not accept this miracle as the incarnation of God in human flesh. Muslims are closer to Jews in the sense that God does not reveal himself in human flesh and hence Jesus was not the only messiah.

"Allah" is the Arabic word for God and refers to the God of Moses, Jesus and Muhammad. In fact, Islam recognizes Jesus as a prophet, though not the son of God. In the case of Christianity, many in keeping with the Nicene Creed are Trinitarians with a belief in a tripartite (but simultaneously single) God – God the father, His son and the Holy Spirit. Of course, Christians are divided on whether the father and the son are equal as well as the full divinity of the Holy Spirit. Whether the spirit is a force; "that holy influence of God' or a person.

Islam reveres both the Old and New Testaments as integral parts of its tradition. However, Muslims generally believe that those texts in current form have been tampered with by man. Both faiths impose a moral code on believers, which varies from a fairly rigid proscription for fundamentalists to relatively relaxed guidelines for liberals. Notwithstanding, there is a strong concern by both the Islamic and Christian traditions for correct behavior.

Although they have some beliefs in common with Christians, Muslims are guided by the teachings of the Quran (which Muslims believe was revealed to Muhammad,) and the Sunnah (or the way of the Prophet that is, the collected sayings or *hadith*, and the deeds of the seventh century Prophet Muhammad). The Bible is the sacred text for Christians revealed by God to the prophets, including Moses. However, some Christians, even those who claim "solo scriptura" emphasis supplements to the Bible, for example, the Church of Latter Day Saints – the Book of Mormon, and Seventh-day Adventists – Ellen White's God-inspired writings.

Muslims see Muhammad as the last in a long line of prophets preceded by Abraham, Moses and Jesus. These three are referenced in the Quran. Christians, however, view Jesus not as a mere prophet, but as a God-man, and the redeemer of this world – a superhuman figure.

Like all other world religions, including Christianity, certain dogma (or set of beliefs) and rituals characterized Islam. The seven basic beliefs of Islam are the existence of God, angels, revealed scripture, prophets, the Day of Judgment, the supremacy of divine will, and life after death. The primary rituals are called the five pillars of the faith: Shahadah (declaration of faith), Salaat (prayers), Zakat (charitable or welfare contributions), Hajj (pilgrimage to Mecca), and Sawm Ramadan (fasting during the month of Ramadan).

Muslims pray to God facing Mecca five times a day. These prayer times are believed to set the rhythm of the day. They not only connect each worshipper to God but to other Muslims around the world. Muslims make charitable donations that require them to give 2.5 percent of their wealth for certain purposes in the cause of God, such as to assist the needy and sponsor missionary work. This is comparable to the tithe or 10 percent of one's income associated with many Christian faiths. In doing Zakat, or purification of wealth, Muslims believe that in addition to helping the poor, they are freeing themselves from the love of possessions and greed.

Muslims also undertake the Hajj. This pilgrimage is an annual event that takes place in the 12th month of the lunar year, but only those who are physically and financially able are required to do so. And before doing so, pilgrims must ensure that their families are taken care of while they are away.

During the month of Ramadan, which marks the revelation of the Quran to the Prophet Muhammad, Muslims fast, a practice and discipline not foreign to Christians. The month of fasting takes place during the ninth month of the Islamic calendar – which is lunar, not solar – and lasts for 29 to 30 days, during which time the fast is dawn to sunset. The purpose of the fast is to ask for God's forgiveness and show appreciation for the blessings and opportunities that He has provided. By fasting, the Muslim is reaffirming his or her commitment to serve God.

While these ritualistic pillars of faith or tasks separate Islam from Christianity, both religions grew out of the same part of the world – the Middle East – and hold forth one God and trace their roots to Abraham.

Like many other believers, Muslims have a special day of the week in which congregational worship is emphasized. Muslims regard Friday as the day for community prayer and teaching. However, Muslims do not consider Friday a holy day in which work should be avoided. On the other hand, many Christians and Jews hold in high regard a holy day – either Sunday (the Lord's Day) or Saturday (the Sabbath).

Then again, both Islam and Christianity adhere to the afterlife and God's two-sided judgment. That man should not be lulled into a sense of security and be oblivious to what the future holds. Every simple everyday act of mercy and kindness will not go unnoticed. For God, everything has meaning in the ultimate scheme of things. Coming soon is a "day of the Lord" or the end-time intervention with its restorative justice.

Like nonorthodox Christians, which are broadly divided between Catholics and Protestants, Muslim believers are divided into a variety of sects, the two major branches being the Sunnis and Shiites. These divisions are primarily due to different interpretations of the Quran and the life experience of Muhammad, resulting in antagonism between the members, just as there are religious rivalries within and among Christian denominations, resulting in schisms. Within Western Christianity, Martin Luther, the German Catholic monk who was excommunicated, may have started a trend that has resulted in the proliferation of Protestant denominations, similar to the case of Islam.

It is a natural phenomenon for people to prefer spending time with others who are similar. Many Christians feel comfortable with people who believe similarly, and share the same values. However, if Christians are to be proficient and more effective in their witness, they are well advised to better follow Jesus' example by moving outside their comfort zones; mingle with and better understand Muslims and Islam.

Here is the challenge. How do Christians balance the injunction to "come out of her, my people" with the directive to follow Christ's example in mingling and "desiring the good of others." How will we know when we get the right balance?

In large measure, many Christians do well to broaden their understanding of other people and cultures, including Islam. By so doing, they are likely to have a greater sensitivity about how other people live in the universe and experience faith.

Seventh-day Adventists Vote to Maintain Status Quo

VI Daily News, August 8, 2015: 24 and 26;
St. Croix Avis, August 9-11, 2015: 8.

S EVENTH-DAY ADVENTISTS, ONE of the most rapidly growing Protestant, religious denominations in the world, is fast changing its size, now 18 million members in 190 countries, but not its fundamentalist identity and belief systems. Fundamentalists far too often view change as "change for the worse."

Fundamentalism is a conservative, religious set of doctrines that generally oppose or are in tension with intellectualism/science and worldly accommodation – what are regarded as the popular vices or amusements such as smoking, gambling and the like – in favor of protecting and/or restoring traditional ways of thinking and behaving.

These are agreed upon at the inception and often derived from a literal and as some put it "a narrow interpretation" of the sacred text.

The progressive strand within its ranks recently locked horns with the conservatives at the 60ᵗʰ General Conference in July in Port Antonio, Texas, a meeting that Adventists hold only once every five years. One of the major events was not specifically whether women should be ordained as ministers. Rather it was whether each division of the church – such as the conference with headquarters in St. Croix – should have the right, on its own, to decide on the issue.

This world body has been resisting efforts to ordain women to the ministry for decades. Notwithstanding, certain conferences of Adventists in the United States and Europe have long seen a need and voted for women like men to be "consecrated and set apart for sacred tasks." It is said in some quarters that the prohibition against women is holding back their ability to function in a modern culture, that it is a barrier for young people and that it may border on discrimination – ironically in a faith where Ellen White, a woman, is its spiritual founder and pillar and is revered as a prophetess whose writings hold para-biblical authority.

On the other hand, proponents of the status quo read scripture as banning women from overseeing men. Divine ideology dictates that women are not formally qualified to lead at the apex. Women can be elders, senior ones too, and deaconesses and can be involved in the decision-making process. but never full-time, bona fide, salaried ordained ministers.

In defiance, North American Adventists have voted for women to be ordained, and in the largest U.S. conference, in South California, where Loma Linda University, one of its medical schools, is located, Sandra E. Roberts was not only ordained but elected president in 2013.

However, the church's top executive body, led by Ted Wilson, who was recently unanimously re-elected as president of the world church, has tended to take the "don't ask; don't tell approach."

This position doesn't appear to be immutable because unlike in previous years, Adventists allow women to be "commissioned" and serve as de-facto ministers, though it has never officially allowed for diverse practices on an issue as fundamental as this.

At this year's General Conference, the delegates voted 977 in favor and 1,381 opposed to the motion for women to be ordained as ministers/priests. Though the current policy was retained, this suggests that there was a fair amount of collateral damage. Hence, the issue may be far from settled.

Hard-line fundamentalists, when in the ascendancy, are never in haste to compromise and alter their position. Changes are going to be embraced – but slowly and at a point when the majority is on board to avert segmentation.

In 1950, just one-third of Adventists were in Africa and Latin America; today, it's more like 80 percent and it is where most of the resistance to the ordination of women resides. Just more than 1 million of the 18 million world-wide live in the United States, where its members, along with those in Europe, are more amenable to change. What the vote ostensibly did was maintain global church unity and avert the possibility of a split, quite apart from the argument that such a weighty issue ought to be based not on popularity but biblical purity.

Another important set of decisions at the General Conference, which drew 60,000 to 70,000 people, were amendments to some of the standing 28 fundamental beliefs. The church reaffirmed a belief that God created the world in seven days as precisely described in the Genesis account.

This issue, which touches on academic freedom and external accreditation, has come up in some Adventist colleges and universities, as it has at other conservative Christian institutions of higher learning.

Alternative scientific approaches or the word "day" as symbolic are seen as watering down personal faith and ignoring the unexplainable mysteries associated with religion, outside the realm of science.

Coming on the heels of the U.S. Supreme Court's decision to legalize same-sex marriage in all 50 states, the church did not shy away and agreed to an edit of the Adventist doctrine that refers in places to a commitment between "partners." The new language makes it clear that same-sex marriage is against Adventist practice and marriage is between one man and one woman. There are of course LGBT Adventists but these are very much on the fringe.

Few doubt that religious patterns are changing and that reasonable people can disagree on what is right and wrong within biblical parameters. Conservatives tend to view any change, including the ordination of women as ministers as a slippery slope and a mark of moral decline or drift, not substantiated in scripture. Progressives view the establishment as rigid and self-righteous. Select changes are seen as liberation from the all-encompassing beliefs of the past, giving members more choices about what to believe and practice, all in accordance with the sacred text.

It is left to be seen whether the worldwide demographic shifts within the Seventh-day Adventist church – which has a substantial and growing membership in the Virgin Islands and the wider Caribbean will, in the coming years, continue to harbor a negative view of the ordination of women to be ministers of the gospel and correspondingly regard the ordination debate as a form of secular feminism.

Or will there be an increase in the number of members who will deem the equalizing of gender roles for ministry as appropriate, harmless, inclusive and adding to its thrust to advance the cause of God?

Spiritual Winds Are Blowing

VI Daily News, January 8, 1987: 6.

T HERE IS A wind of spiritual change currently blowing through the U.S. Virgin Islands. This force is the upsurge of the evangelical and charismatic renewals in the Christian church today.

Yesteryear, fundamentalists were not only marginal but an invisible religious aggregate. However, in recent times, they have gained considerable importance. Present-day politicians are known to woo their vote more than ever before.

Concrete manifestations of this spiritual wind was noticeable on the occasion of world-renowned gospel singer Andrea Crouch's visit to our shores in November.

This famous singing evangelist electrified the Reichhold Center with his velvet voice and the spiritual message in the songs he sang. I suspect that this was the case at other venues where he and supporting artists appeared in the Virgin Islands.

The unprecedented wave of converts to evangelicalism in recent years among the descendants of the enslaved who were brought to the Caribbean is in contrast with the time when people principally flocked to the Catholic, Lutheran, Episcopalian, Moravian and other mainline churches.

The "born-agains" are seen in their hundreds in worship on Sundays and Saturdays. More and more of their churches dot the territory.

Evidence of the growing strength of this aggregate is exhibited in their decision to band together to own and operate WGOD, a Christian radio station where the church's music is often aired.

No wonder people turned out in large numbers to see their star. These personalities have outdone their reggae counterparts. Internationally acclaimed Bob Marley never performed in the Virgin Islands.

On the occasion of Crouch's final concert in the territory, it was a proud moment when local artistes West Pemberton and Shirley Pemberton-White and the Pemberton singers, as well as the Flight, prepared the way and made the ambience just right for the main act of the evening.

The whole place shook us with the power of a mighty, rushing wind when the talented Crouch came on stage after being introduced by Radio and TV personality Addie Ottley. The nine-member team of melodious voices replete with tambourine, drums, piano, organ - although stentorian at times - proclaimed the good news of the risen Lord.

Crouch sang his soul out. So enthralled was his being that the beads of perspiration covered him like a hard worker in a vineyard. It must have been an ecstatic occasion on the Day of Pentecost some 2,000 years ago when Peter so captivated his listeners that they clapped their hands, sang and rejoiced over the news of an ascended Savior. So too was the joy and sober merriment of the early Christians at Antioch, in Rome, and wherever the converts of Paul and the disciples carried the good news of Jesus Christ.

They were few in attendance whose spirits were not moved and whose hands and feet were not showing the mighty power of a risen Christ.

When the time came, Crouch, who has had to defend a charge of drug abuse, spoke of his witness for Jesus and the moment of his conversion. His music and the enthusiasm of his colleagues in his singing ministry supported that assertion. It is difficult to find a singer or group to render "Jesus is the Answer" as mellifluously as does Andrea Crouch.

But hold it. Crouch's fame has brought him a plethora of critics. Many of his provocateurs spring from the very Christian community of which he is allegedly a part.

His detractors dub his performance beyond the pale of religious music. He is seen as "a wolf in sheep's clothing" who has been suckered in by the luring commercialism of Hollywood. Many purists find much of his music bordering on the sacrilegious and would not pay a dime to hear him.

Whatever merit there may be in the claim of Crouch's vulgarization of religious music, the occasion spoke for itself. It seems to be "a gathering of God's people."

We are quick to talk about our youth's indulgence with illicit drugs; becoming embroiled in various forms of criminality; falling prey to teenage pregnancy and other entanglements.

I have no doubt that some and far too many use drugs, as well as engage in other "popular vices" and are harmed by such practices.

However, we tend to forget or ignore the fact that in the territory and beyond there is an even larger number of decent young people, and older folks too, who are hooked not on drugs, but on Jesus Christ.

These stewards have found a new way of living. They are cheerful and joyful, if not happy, in extolling the name of Jesus. Irrespective of human frailty, these individuals, many of whom hail from the lower strata, follow Christ in their daily lives, eschewing drugs and other blandishments associated with an intense secular life style

Note worthily, these burgeoning other-world oriented Christians are not merely a moral force but seemingly wield considerable political power.

No wonder that pro-business Gov. Alexander Farrelly, who has promulgated his hope to govern the V.I. into the 1980s, is politically prudent to discourage casino gambling. In his own words, "The churches would murder us."

Such an admission, along with the strategic role of key church officials in the settlement of the strike on the eve of the 1986 election, bespeak the clout of the Christian community in V.I. society.

"Born agains," who are typically status quo-oriented, are more than patrons of gospel music, they are a vital part of the political arena in the Virgin Islands and serve as grist for the political machine.

~

Preaching with a Calypso Beat

VI Daily News, April 2, 2016: 22-23.

During the last two weeks or so, there has been a very rustic-looking (though conspicuous) tent that has attracted the attention of passers-by along the Donoe by-pass, across from the Home Depot on the island of St. Thomas. Some who traverse this road look askance and go they merry way. Others are curious enough to be part of the great multitude of Virgin Islanders who routinely spend over two hours at a time at night at this spot, often after a tiring and exhausting work day.

They come in the hundreds and "full-up" the 1,500 seating capacity venue. Scores are seen standing on the outside peering in. Among this throng are those who even trek by ferry from the neighboring island of St. John. They meet five days out of the seven-day week. The only respite for these dear souls is Monday and Thursday nights. It seems not to matter that they sacrifice two solid hours of the pleasures of prime-time television and other mundane pursuits.

I glean that this white-and-yellow colored tent was not mounted with camping or any other such recreational activities in mind, but for the purpose of conducting evangelical services. Paradoxically, those who are found under its canopy appear to be having lots of fun. The gatherings, largely composed of immigrants from the Eastern Caribbean, enjoy sermons replete with anecdotes and jokes that are nostalgic, elicit laughter, and even thunderous clapping normally associated with stand-up comedy. However, coupled with the hilarity and the skillful use of dialect, all part of religious innovation, these tools are seemingly meant to make religious activities more relevant and culturally-sensitive to congregants - to attract millennials and outsiders to the sober business of the re-creation of individual self-awareness.

They come out in droves to hear the charismatic, visiting man of God, Claudius Morgan, a native from St. Vincent in the Eastern Caribbean, who has preached the word of God the world over, including Africa, Asia, Latin America and throughout the Caribbean. This is the 130th outing or 5-week crusade under his belt, this one dubbed the "Good News Gospel Explosion" He not only tickles the intellectual curiosity expounding on his own version of the teaching of truth that "Jesus is the Way," but also gets his audience to decide to follow Him.

From its inception, recruitment into the army of God in the market place for souls is the constant and underlying objective for the proclamation of the gospel in Christian churches. However, the manner in which this goal is enacted has radically changed over the years and evangelist Morgan is an apparent example of this religious innovation. This is a pattern that has taken hold among both Roman Catholics (post-Vatican II) and Protestants, particularly among Pentecostals. The promotion of the core values of the gospel message to counter the secularization that has become so prevalent in the developed world and even the emerging societies like the Caribbean, including the Virgin Islands, are the same but the packaging is different.

The religious heritage of Caribbean people includes the social formations which range from Cuban Santeria, through Shango and Spiritual Baptists in Trinidad to Haitian Vodun, Pocomania and Rastafarianism in Jamaica – all Afro-Caribbean syncretisms. However, many of the Christian denominations with which the majority of the Caribbean masses and others have affiliated, like the Roman Catholics and the Episcopalians, have been cradled and headquartered in the European metropolis, external to the Caribbean - in such places as Rome; Kent, United Kingdom. The Moravians, who were the first to work among the enslaved in St. Thomas, Virgin Islands, arrived from Germany.

The Mormons and the Seventh-day Adventists are North American in origin.

Hence, for a long time, the resident leaders of this colonial religious outpost were expatriates and foreign to the region. A lot of this pattern has changed and evangelist Morgan is part of the ongoing Caribbeanization, not only of the clergy but the liturgy of God's church here on earth.

Unlike many Caribbean professionals who receive appropriate training in metropolitan countries prior to returning to their homeland to serve, Morgan is Caribbean-trained, having received his degree in theology from the University of the Southern Caribbean in Trinidad which provide a seminary-type experience for future Seventh-day Adventists or clergy. Moreover, his personal history as a former calypsonian in his native St. Vincent and across the sub-region has apparently rendered his homiletic style, phonetic tone and anecdotal content of his sermonizing to be radically different from many of his colleagues and predecessors. This includes fellow union evangelist K.S. Wiggins who took St. Thomas by storm and garnered 303 converts in 1973 in a similar crusade right here in St. Thomas.

Unlike many of his colleagues, who tend to emulate foreign models and whose impression management, including homilies, are therefore not quite as culturally relevant, Morgan is an example of religious innovation or the effort to change existing approaches, to better meet current needs. If the proof of the pudding is in the eating, Morgan may be a trend-setter and part of a new wave of Caribbean-style preachers. With the strategy of "each one, win one", Morgan has crusade-by-crusade added thousands of new converts to the Church of God and for inclusion in his resume.

With the God-given talent he brings to the craft, his appeal is like magic as he unveils his messages intermingled with pulsating calypso-flavored dance and song. The smug and the stiff who eschew clapping and laughter in sacred spaces might shy away from his light-hearted and jocular approach, forthrightness, candor and transparency. The audience may well be reminded of the playwright William Shakespeare "All the world a stage" in his comedy <u>As you Like It</u>. While on stage, Morgan's religio-theatrical performances, in term of style and the presentation of self, are every bit like that of a calypsonian in a tent. The body language, the spontaneous and improvised singing, long associated with kaiso singing or storytelling, are the hooks that are used to revert to, or invoke, the principles and conformity exacted by "the old-time religion." It is transparently clear that Sabbath observance, tithing and the sanctity of traditional marriage are high on his list, not to mention The Three Angels Messages and the Sanctuary.

Now in its third week, I visited this place of celebration of Jesus. It seems as though a thousand voices were singing in unison "I don't want to be left out" and, of course, this quest for inclusion is not the imminent St. Thomas Carnival or the popular Afternoon on the Green at the University of the Virgin Islands, but the other-world experience or the Kingdom of God. These folk, many of whom, I am told "have washed their robes in the blood of the Lamb" were in religious solidarity as they praised God in song and "Majesty." The old, young, the halt, the lame and I even glimpsed a blind woman, all sang with relish "Draw me close to you and never let me go." They even asked the Almighty to "help *them* find *their* way" in an amorphous, bewildering and fast-paced changing world.

The Caribbean Church is the better for producing men of God who are willing to make Christianity more culturally relevant – preachers like the former calypsonian, turned gospel preacher, Claudius Morgan. It may be that the Caribbean religious elite lose sight of the fullness of its mission if and when, even with good intentions, it maintains the status quo; cast aside religious innovation and are all too ready and comfortable to operate like clones of their metropolitan progenitors. Even though God is constant, the social psychology of Caribbean people and the culture in which they are embedded are unique and different, and so must those who address the spiritual needs of its people. Traditional or mainstream preaching has its place but the Caribbean-centered style as exemplified in the Morgan model is a breath of fresh air and one which apparently resonates with Caribbean folk. In addition to the fact that it allows for diversity in the proclamation of the gospel, the litmus test to determine its viability and long-term efficiency may well, in the long run, reside in the possibility of its replication as well as the retention rate of converts.

Morgan's success as a *fisher of men* appears to have so far silenced his detractors and critics. Where ever he goes, this born-again Calypso preacher draws thousands to the Word of God as well as into "the ark of safety" and the Virgin Islands are no exception.

CHOICES: CARNIVAL AND THE CHURCH

VI Daily News, April 5, 2017: 29.

CARNIVAL, A FESTIVAL in almost each island of the Caribbean archipelago, comes once a year, though it is scheduled at different times.

The birthplace of reggae, Jamaica; holds its increasingly soca-filled Carnival in late April. Modern Carnival also finds its way to Nassau in early May, although the traditional Bahamian Junkanoo Parade is still held in December. Lucian Carnival, originally before the Lenten season, is now held in mid-July. In Barbados, the festival that historically celebrated success in harvesting crops is appropriately called "Crop Over," and bridges late July and early August. Grenada's Spicemas Festival follows a week later. In Antigua and Barbuda, their celebration comes in mid-August. In St. Kitts and Nevis, hundreds trek home to witness and participate in what seems like a Christmas Carnival.

Putting Brazil's Carnival and Mardi Gras in New Orleans, La., aside, the mother of all Carnivals and the biggest Caribbean attraction on the yearly calendar is found in Trinidad and Tobago during the month of February – after which all others have been modeled, though each festival has its own unique features. Locally, in the three-island territory of the United States Virgin Islands, it is plainly called the St. Thomas Carnival and comes in April.

So compelling and infectious are this Caribbean event, with its nostalgic pull, that it has extended and reproduced itself in the diaspora. It is a magnet for immigrants in such places as Great Britain, it is London's Nothing Hill Carnival; and Metropolitan Toronto has its own version called Caribana – both occurring weeks apart in August. For those in New York City, all roads lead to the Eastern Parkway in Brooklyn where the West Indian Day Parade is held on Labor Day in September.

This festival is seen by some as a big plus. Many immigrants schedule return visits to their native lands to engage in merriment, reconnect with their roots, and network with friends. Along with systematic remittances, this serves as an injection of revenue so badly needed to buoy the economies. Carnival also acts as an outlet or safety valve for those at home to release pent-up disaffection with a myriad of issues – ranging from island politics to the alarming rise of crime rates to personal woes – by engaging in mass rituals of non-revolutionary celebration.

However, because the peoples of the socio-cultural area have had an ongoing love affair with and ambivalence to Carnival, and its adhesion, the calypso, it has attracted its own share of controversy, with some persons questioning whether Christians should be involved in such activities.

The situation has not been helped by the lack of a common position taken by the church on this matter. On one hand, given the varying approaches to the Bible, there are Christians who participate in Carnival in various ways. Members of the clergy on various isles have actually been part of bands or troops. In one case, a Catholic priest made news for attempting to lead a troop on Kadooment Day, the culmination of Barbados' Crop Over. Some opine that to frown on either adult or children's parades – with their breathtaking, colorful masquerades – is to make an enemy of the good that can also come from such celebrations. Along these lines, Carnival is seen by some as inherently beneficial to the life and vitality of the community. In a socially-stratified and class-conscious society as is the Caribbean, Carnival is a leveling mechanism that provides opportunities for the people from various walks of life – to come together as one to express creativity, and hence a positive contribution to social cohesion. Yes, there may be bad elements, including internecine crime, excessive alcohol consumption, the drunkenness to go with the revelry; but the festival as a whole is beneficial and cannot be blamed on account of individuals who abuse the situation.

On the other hand, there are some Christians (and other conservative thinkers) who categorically see Carnival as part of the secularization and corruption of the society, as well as the commercialization of an event with religious roots. In specific terms, this point of view contends that Carnival, which has moved away from its religious origins, has become commercialized, and moreover contributes to the moral decay and lawlessness that has become rampant. They would therefore urge fellow believers to keep away from such "evil influences."

It is proffered that the spirit behind the Carnival has its origin in the sacred text or Bible – though not the present form and substance, which differ from culture to culture. The Feast of the Tabernacles (ingathering or booths) is one of the three great Jewish festivals and it is this which corresponds to today's Carnival. In biblical times; the festival has both historic and an agricultural significance. This event served as a reminder to the Jews that there was a time when they were homeless wanderers in the dessert without a roof over their heads. So the law was laid down that for seven days people would live in booths or stalls erected along the streets or in the gardens. The booths were made of boughs of trees and branches of palms. This event was the most popular of the Jewish festivals, and also referred to as "the season of gladness."

New World slavery certainly had an undeniable influence on Carnival and calypso. Songs were sung by captured Africans aboard slave ships on their journey from Africa to the Caribbean. For the enslaved that worked on plantations often used songs to distract while performing grueling work on the sugarcane fields; at functions among themselves; and especially during Christmas. When the songs were sung in the work fields, it made the work seemingly bearable and less arduous. Such songs were sung again when the slaves met to celebrate the cutting of the sugarcane to thank God for the harvest, with its obvious religious connotation. One such calypso that demonstrates this connection, made popular by singer and actor Harry Belafonte, is "Day-O, (day-o, daylight come and we want to go home.)" Consequently, one salient feature of the Carnival's schedule of events is the Calypso tent with its singing and monarch competitions, part of the heritage and patrimony of Caribbean people.

Notwithstanding it being one of its core values and indigenous to the Caribbean, calypso has long been on the edge of society's standards of decency. Potentially a mass and effective educational tool, cariso or the calinda song along, with soca – its derivative – are emblematic of the talented and larger-than-life figures in Caribbean society. One example is Francisco Slinger, better known as the Mighty Sparrow, a Trinidadian born in Grenada and a Caribbean household name. For his genius as a calypsonian, an honorary Doctor of Letters degree was conferred by the University of the West Indies – just one of his many accolades for his mastery of this art form. Hollis Liverpool, better known as the Mighty Chalkdust, a fellow Trinidadian, once part of the teaching faculty at the University of the Virgin Islands and now of the University of the Trinidad and Tobago, has shied away from smut calypso. His composition, "Learn from Arithmetic," with its refrain, "75 can't go into 14," won him the 2017 Monarch title for the ninth time, breaking Sparrow's record. It is an example of conscious-awareness commentary on child marriage or old men having relationships with young girls.

Though Sparrow's "Education" is a classic of what is good about calypso, "Salt Fish," with its double entendre, is far more transparent and felt by the prudish to be beyond the pale and better left unsung. From all of this discourse has spun "Gospel Calypso," ostensibly a sanitized or puritanical version of the art form; along with the "high sounding cymbal" is now embraced by the Pentecostal and charismatic tendencies of the faith with the proviso of its God-centered lyrics, though the dance-provoking beat is the same.

Carnival and calypso have become part of the tourism-branding of the Caribbean and seen as a viable option for earnings going forward. The Association of Caribbean States created the Caribbean Carnival Network on July 6, 2015 in Santiago de Cuba and the Baranquilla Carnival Foundation has proposed to host the First Meeting on Caribbean Culture in Mexico in May, in hopes of strengthening sustainable and cultural tourism in the Greater Caribbean. The Virgin Islands, with its emphasis on cruise-tourism, will do well to become a signatory of this network that includes Cuba, the Bahamas, Dominican Republic, Colombia, Grenada, Haiti, Trinidad and Tobago, and even Martinique – a French Overseas Territory.

However, over the years, charges of vulgar behavior and general dispossession of morals associated with Carnival have been leveled by religious leaders at this still evolving Caribbean festival. This has led many people to take the posture that the Christian Church and Carnival do not mix; that the festival, at its core, is an indulgence not for Christians; a celebration at which many understandably cringe and from which they feel the need to stay away.

Some purport that while the church would not raise an eyebrow at bland events like the St. Thomas Carnival Food Fair and the children-centered Coney Island activities, it is challenging to separate things in the same basket. The purists contend that when the festival is judged as a whole, it boasts vulgar behavior; calypso lyrics that are sometimes "smutty and degrading of women"; and sometimes lascivious and lewd dances ("whining" or "*wukking* up") that are accompanied by pulsating music rhythms. This, for the purist, is reprehensible. Such severe structural and deep-seated changes, very possibly changing the entire dynamic of Carnival, would have to be implemented to allow conscientious and conservative Christian participation. That, it is argued, is a fight not worth having. It is akin to placing plasters on weeping sores.

All Christians and others agree, regardless of the differences in doctrines, that the biggest cultural event in the Caribbean, including in St. Thomas, is Carnival, larger than any sporting event, not to mention church-related events. Where the disagreements arise is over whether Christians should participate or maintain their distance from this festival.

So it would seem that various denominations of the Christian faith – but also the Muslim, Jewish, Bobo Ashanti and other faiths – have varying views on whether there is a place for the church or religion in Carnival; and to what extent the church and/or its adherents should be involved. Some church leaders and their parishioners agree that Carnival is compatible with the Christian lifestyle and should not be unconditionally disparaged. Hence, they lend tacit and other support; seemingly and unwittingly increasing their participation. Others, though they have possibly come around to embrace the "steel pan" music with its artistry and infectious calypso beat in church services, view Carnival as outside of their comfort zone and continue to regard this undisputable popular festival as something to be shunned.

It is possible to enjoy Carnival without compromising one's faith? There are undoubtedly many who continue to participate in Carnival festivities, while claiming to maintain a personal connection to their God and church; others regard it as something to be shunned. And so, the argument seesaws back and forth.

The Mystery of Evil

VI Daily News, April 22, 2017: 20 & 22.

ONE OF THE perennial and puzzling questions in Christian theology is: If God exists and is good, and is so loving and so powerful, why is there so much suffering in the world, especially when it happens to good people This question has baffled students and scholars of the bible as long as "the good book" existed. Indeed, this enigma has at best fostered doubt among some, and at worst cemented atheism among many.

Moreover, it is not the supposed scientific evidence vis-à-vis religious dogma in general, or the alleged overwhelming data supporting evolution, in particular, which, I suggest, causes atheists to reject God. It is this problem of evil. So the logic goes: If God is so good and all powerful as He is purported to be, He would certainly do something about evil – if He really exists. Hence, atheist philosopher J.L. Mackie claims that if God exist, there would be no evil at all.

There is not only the reality of evil, but also the extent and magnitude of "man's inhumanity to man." Atheist William Rowe has argued that God's existence is inconsistent with pointless and gratuitous evil. Seen as blasphemy by some, the ancient Greek philosopher, Epicurus threw up his hands in despair at solving the problem of evil by asking his famous series of questions: First, "Is God willing to prevent evil, but not able?" Then He is impotent; Second, "Is God able, but not willing?" Then He is malevolent. Third, "Is He both able and willing? Then, why the problem? In other words, if we look at the characteristics commonly ascribed to God in theistic philosophy, we find some apparent contradictions. For if God is all powerful, all-knowing and all-loving, then why have a world with so much evil or with any at all?

Christian philosophers, like Stephen Wykstra, Peter van Inwagen and Stephen Cowen, who have produced critiques of the atheists' work on the problem of evil, have given us a justification for the existence of evil in a world created by a good and benevolent God. Theodicy is the defense of God's goodness in view of the existence of evil.

The conventional response to the existence of such demonstrations of evil, as torture and other heinous crimes, is that the free-will of humans cause this type of suffering. In other words, because God has given human beings free moral agency, heartless individuals are able to rape and engage in mass murder and suicide bombings. Moreover, because we have freedom to drink, get drunk, and still drive, we can under the influence of alcohol kill other human beings. In other words, by God not making us robots and by giving humans free-will, this allows for evil. Put differently, mankind could not have free will without the possibility of evil.

God, says Christian philosophers, would have to intervene and interrupt the freedom of human beings every time they attempt to do wrong in order to have a world without evil. Fundamentally, freedom is very important to God as it is to humans. This argument seems very impressive to many and has been employed by some of the greatest philosophers in Christian history. Most philosophers of religion credit Alvin Plantinga with providing the decisive refutation of the logical problem of evil.

Christians also purport that individuals often go through suffering in their lives as a means of building character and becoming better persons. Many individuals, even non-Christians and others, will, in retrospect, vouch that it was good for them to have been subjected to a certain period of suffering or to have experienced deprivation, some hardship or even calamity. It helped to develop strength in them that they never knew they had - out of adversity can come opportunity - and that as a consequence of suffering, they are the better for it. God's glory is served even when evil is permitted. Genesis records the story of Joseph's brothers selling him into slavery. Though Joseph suffered tragically from the evil done by his brothers, at the end of the story, Joseph rose to prominence in Egypt. Of course, the most significant example is the evil murder of Jesus Christ which Christians believe resulted in the salvation of the world. In these cases, God has a morally sufficient reason for allowing evil – to bring about a greater good.

John Kick dubbed this "soul-making theodicy." God is purifying his creatures – like gold in the crucible of the refiner's fire. This argument in favor of evil is that there is almost always some redeeming lesson, virtue or good which comes from episodes of suffering. That's laudable for those who benefit from such experiences, but what of those who succumb to evil and are burnt up. There are many people who suffer horrendous evils and with no apparent benefit to them, this side of heaven.

Keith Yandell asserts that there is nothing in Christian beliefs about God that would lead one to expect that God must ensure that a person's experience in this life be worthwhile for that person. We must look at the totality of life which extends far beyond the mortal experience. Yandell concludes that "if life extends at least indefinitely beyond the grave ... then when the totality of life is examined, it may well turn out that life was, overall, worthwhile."

What have we to say about nature as the cause of evil or "natural" evil, which Christians contend is under the control of the Almighty God? There is evil that occurs not because some human was expressing free will, but evil caused by earthquakes, hurricanes, tsunamis, flooding or other natural events. Critics query: Why couldn't the Almighty prevent these so-called "acts of God" without compromising the issue of free-will?

Obviously, free-will or human-made evil does not come into play here. Free-will is not violated when natural disasters result in personal injury, destruction of property or even death. No doubt, evil brought on by nature may continue to prolong the age of doubt, the more so when we are reminded that Christians teach that God can perform miracles. Why not one to avert natural evil?

In addition to free-will and nature, Christians believe that evil is caused by the devil and by extension the fallen state of man/woman. Evil is not God's fault. It is the fault of Adam and Eve who sinned, a state/ weakness or tendency inherited or passed to man as a result of the transmission of original sin. We see this in the case of the story of Job, when the sons of men (or angels) came to see God in Heaven. Satan, who has been roaming the earth as he does today, comes and ultimately inflicts suffering on Job, a righteous man, God having permitted it to occur.

Did Adolph Hitler murder 6 million Jews because he had a strained relationship with his father, an example of evil as learned behavior? Or does an evil gene exist? In their materialist approach to understanding evil, DNA researchers have uncovered the *MAO*-A gene that is linked to anti-social or aggressive behavior. In related studies, Kent A. Kiehl found that there is less density in the para limbic system of a psychopath's brain – the area that processes emotions.

The fact that human beings can't see a reason for God allowing evil does not mean a reason does not exist. Evil is more complicated than our human observation can untangle. Skeptical theism argues that human beings are cognitively limited and cannot know all the plausible, possible reasons why God would permit evil.

Immersed as we are in a world of sin and suffering, it is hard for humans to ultimately understand evil – we see through a glass dimly. However, when this terrible experience with sin or the fallen state has passed, humans will be able to see God's goodness in his dealings with humanity, sin and evil.

Because of God's democratic governance, He is dealing with sin and evil in the best way possible. Some things are simply outside the ken of our epistemic capacity as humans. In fact, there are some evils which might seem unjustifiable and unfathomable from the mind or point of view of finite creatures. People are underserving of their unearned suffering. Conversely, an omnipresent God would have reasons that we humans can't comprehend. It may not be possible to explain evil in a rational and logical manner that is consistent with a reasonable understanding of God's character.

There will come a point in the history of this planet and hopefully in our lives, when praise will be given to God, even if all our questions about evil are unanswered on this side of eternity. Knowing this full-well, evil is not a sufficient reason or excuse to disbelieve in God. The bible teaches that God will one day eradicate evil from His creation. Hence, Christians are called to glorify God in suffering. And in the end, Christians believe, as underscored in Rev. 21:4, that God has prepared an eternal home where there will be no more suffering.

Where Was God in Irma and Maria?

VI Daily News, October 7, 2017: 18 & 22.

T HEY HAVE BEEN variously dubbed a "double whammy". Two massive hurricanes, Irma on the 6th and Maria, 14 days later, on the 20th September 2017, both of which struck with unprecedented fury the U.S. Virgin Islands (USVI), along with other Caribbean islands and south Florida.

In the case of the USVI, these twin Category 5 hurricanes are reportedly associated with the death of at least 4 persons, including a Virgin Islands National Guard soldier, created displaced residents, caused untold damage to property and the islands' infrastructure. These happenings have, among other things, wrought untold suffering and correspondingly produced questions for the religious, including the mainline Christian denominations, the evangelicals and Rasta.

Workers, home owners and other helping hands have been busy ever since fixing and cleaning. FEMA, an acronym for the Federal Emergency Management Agency, The U.S. Army Corps of Engineers and local agencies like the VI Water and Power Authority are providing relief, including repairing power lines. The VI Territorial Emergency Management Agency, in collaboration with other entities, has promised to re-establish communication channels. The islands were literally cutoff from each other and the wider world.

Almost everyone is endeavoring to straighten out things to regain normalcy. With the many fallen trees and absence of electric power, many, particularly those without that buzzing song coming from a generator, have become "hewers of wood and drawers of water."

Countless ill-fated residents wait for their homes to be inspected, and try to get life back to normal as much as possible. As time elapses, frustration, anger, hurt and pain have pooled together, tiring nerves and stretching the limits of patience.

Apart from the existential concerns of everyday life and taking a phrase from Charles Dickens' classic <u>A Tale of Two Cities</u>, it may be "the best and the worst of times" for those impacted by these two record-breaking hurricanes with winds upward of 180 miles. These natural disasters may have produced a plethora of questions for the religious. The Christian establishment, in particular, has been having a hard time to get their own parishioners and prospects alike, in a largely post-modern world and increasingly secularized society, to heed and take their message and theology seriously.

It is the best of times because there has been a discernible reawakening of religious interests as apocalyptic disasters such as Irma and Maria are want to do. In some quarters, people are turning back to the prophetic messages such as those in the biblical books of Revelation, Jeremiah and Ezekiel. Some have been re-reading Matthew 24 where Jesus predicts the signs of the end of the world, including those in the natural world. Many are convinced that these catastrophes are precisely and manifestly an omen of the "End of time." And that this dual tragedy is an unmistakable warning from God; an encouragement for believers to look up for their "redemption draweth nigh."

Jehovah's Witnesses, Seventh-day Adventists and others are associated with advancing these themes. They are particular to emphasize that such disasters will usher in the beginning of the thousand-year reign or the millennium after the great conflagration or Jesus' return. This season, in the wake of Irma and Maria, may prove to be a bumper time for religious marketers of this strand. Evangelicals, charismatics and others should see their pews being filled with more people being "filled with the spirit"; "coming under the anointing" and being "constrained by the fear of God" as a result of the passage of these two hurricanes.

Among the good to come from the deluge which followed on Friday night, September 30, is that the heavy rain and flooding may have, along with earthly trappings, washed away the sins of the spiritually complacent.

Skeptics of this view are quick to caution "not so fast". Hurricane Gilbert in 1988, Hugo in 1989 and now Irma and Maria in 2017 are a return of more intense storms, like the 1940s and 50s. Moreover, researchers have found a correlation between moisture levels in west Central Africa, the birthplace of many tropical storms. Hence, the causal factor behind Irma and Maria is climate change. Fundamentally, this phenomenon is a transformation in global and regional/Caribbean climate patterns, traceable to the mid of the late 20th Century and onwards, thus resulting in increased levels of atmospheric carbon dioxide that are produced by the man-made use of fossil fuels.

Conversely, it could be the worst of times when questions are raised about the goodness of God in the face of such enormous destruction and suffering as a result of natural disasters, not only in the Caribbean, the United States with Harvey but the world of large, not to mention the recent earthquake in Mexico which claimed upward of 50 lives and counting.

There may be a reason why a natural disaster – otherwise called an "act of God" – poses an apparent challenge to religious belief in a way that even more horrific, man-made evil does not. Terrorism, ethnic cleansing, serial and mass murder, like the recent massacre in Las Vegas, USA, which claimed over 50 lives, are attributed to free-will or man's inhumanity to man. Mankind cannot have freedom without the possibility of evil. Some forget that when the first Europeans arrived in the 15th century, Native Americans numbered in the millions. But by 1900, after centuries of conflict and acts of genocide, the "vanishing

Americans" numbered just 250 thousand. In World War II, Joseph Stalin in the Soviet Union killed in excess of 20 million and Mao Zedong reportedly killed tens of million in China's Cultural Revolution. Recent examples include "black and black crime" - Hutus killing Tutsis in the African nation of Rwanda and the killing of hundreds of thousands of people in the Darfur region of Sudan. The kind of death, destruction and suffering caused by natural disaster pale in insignificance when compared to those caused by man or political repression. And so, why the railing, criticism and questioning of God, in respect of natural disasters like Irma and Maria?

Those who blame suffering on God, especially atheists, claim that, not only does free-will not come into play in the case of natural evil – earthquakes, tsunamis, volcanic explosions, hurricanes and flooding - but that if God is so good and all powerful as He is purported to be, He would stamp out evil and suffering. Better yet, don't Christians teach that God can perform miracles that are able to suspend and circumvent scientific laws as well as natural processes.

Suffering in the world has baffled Christians and non-Christians alike for ages. Some are unable to reconcile suffering in all its sordid forms with the loving God of the bible. Irma and Maria may have thrown up old questions and resurfaced doubts about God. But even though suffering can drive people away from God, what is sure, though, is that many will not allow the suffering to wash or blow away the certainty of their faith.

It is man's attitude toward the inevitability of suffering rather than the suffering itself. Suffering offers God an opportunity to display His power. Based on His type of governance of the universe – His creation and creatures - the Eternal God cannot save anyone from the forces of evil. Not even His own dear son, Jesus Christ, was exempted from suffering when he took on human flesh.

When persons wanted to blame the sins of the parents of the blind man as the reason why he was born blind, Jesus gave a reply: "Neither this man nor his parents have sinned but this happened so that the work of God might be displayed." God is in the storms of life, including Irma and Maria, and will work according to His will and good pleasure.

It is impossible for human beings to logically and fully comprehend the reality of the untold suffering in the world, including that which has come about in the aftermath of Hurricanes Irma and Maria, which are likely to become the twin hurricanes of the century. There are too many unanswered questions. Man's understanding of suffering, whether man-made or naturally induced, is outside the ken of our epistemic capacity as humans – we peer through a glass darkly. Our Father knows "that all things work for good to them that love God" (Romans 8: 28).

The Caribbean Religious Elite

St. Croix Avis, March 1, 1989: 6 & 27.

D URING THE LAST four weeks or so, there has been a very simple-looking, though conspicuous tent that has been commanding the attention of a sizeable number of Virgin Islanders, St. Thomians in particular.

They come in the hundreds, night after night, Saturday included. Some even trek by ferry from the neighboring island of St. John. The only respite for these dear souls is Thursday. It seems not to matter that the pleasures of prime time and cable television are sacrificed.

The "big tent," as it has been dubbed, is located on the outer rim of Lindberg, adjacent to the Kirwan Terrace Elementary School. Though in a densely populated area, badly in need of a park and other such facilities, this tent was not mounted, I don't believe with camping or other such activities in mind but for the purpose of conducting church or better put proselytization. Regardless, those who are found under its canopy seem to be having lots of fun and some are recreated.

Though the nightly congregations are predominantly black and hence fail to reflect the racial composition of the Virgin Islands, this rendezvous seems to be a place where smiling faces are many and the welcome is warm and unaffected.

They come out in droves to hear guest speaker Earl Baldwin, a preacher from Trinidad and Tobago. The early dependence and even clamoring among the descendants of the enslaved for Europeans, Americans and even local whites over their own kith and kin is beginning to recede because of growing nationalistic sentiments and ethnic pride, I suppose. Along with the essential content, the medium, these days, is as much an integral part of "the message" in the eyes of the beholder.

Unlike the evangelists of yesteryear, many of whom were missionaries and "sojourners of the truth," Baldwin seems to be part of a new breed that has come to comprise the Caribbean religious elite. He is a Seventh-day Adventist minister but there are many others like himself who are lodged in both the mainline churches and even among the so-called sects.

The religious heritage of Caribbean people includes unique social inventions which range from Cuban Santeria, through Shango in Trinidad, Haitian Vodun, Pocomania and Rastafarianism in Jamaica. However, many of the Christian denominations with which the majority of the Caribbean masses and others are affiliated, like the Roman Catholics, Jehovah's Witnesses, the Episcopalians, have been cradled and are headquartered external to the Caribbean in such distant places as Rome, New York City and Kent, United Kingdom. The Moravians, who were the first to work among the slaves in St. Thomas, Virgin Islands, arrived from Germany.

Moreover, for a long time, the resident leaders of these colonial religious outposts were expatriates and foreign to the region. A lot of this pattern has changed and evangelist Baldwin, I gather, is a part of the ongoing Caribbeanization of God's church here on earth. Similar to the political arena, the struggle for turf among these men of God did not always come easy and was even ugly at times. It is not yet over and, notwithstanding the appointment of Bishop Barbara Harris, the score on the role of women as clergy has not yet been settled even among Seventh-day Adventists who ironically reserve a singular place for prophetess Ellen White.

Baldwin, who holds a master's degree in theology is "one of we" having been born in the Caribbean. Unlike many Caribbean professionals who received appropriate training in metropolitan countries prior to returning to their homelands to serve, he is Caribbean-trained, having attended Caribbean Union College in Trinidad. His personal history and graduate socialization have apparently rendered his homiletic style, phonetical tone and the anecdotal content of his sermonizing to be different from many of his colleagues, black and white alike, who often emulate and adopt foreign models and whose sermons therefore are not quite as culturally relevant.

With the talent he brings to the craft, his appeal is like "magic" as he unveils his messages with vigor and without fear. One is reminded of the Prophet Jeremiah. The smug and the so-called sophisticated might shy away from his forthrightness.

I made bold to enter this place as they were celebrating. Service was in progress. Immediately, I understood what King David must have meant in his Psalms when he uttered "I would rather be a door-keeper in the house of the Lord than to dwell in tents of wickedness for a season."

It seemed as though a thousand voices were singing in unison "Leaning on the Everlasting Arms." These black folk, many of whom, I am told "have washed their robes in the blood of the Lamb," were carrying on as they praised God in song. The old, young, the halt, the lame and I even glimpsed a blind fellow, all sang with relish and bothered, in an age of science, to call upon the name of the Lord in prayer.

Also, the response that is elicited from the hungry Lindberg multitude by the powerful preaching of Baldwin as he elucidates with remarkable clarity on such profound subjects as The Three Angels' Message and the Sanctuary as outlines in the dense books of Daniel and Revelation belie the fact that the only place earthlings can have fun is by listening to Sister Rita Marley at the Lionel Roberts Stadium or at a fish fry with some good old Cruzan rum. Nothing could be further from the truth.

To all appearances, these people are happy and having fun in a way not thought of before. Moreover, they come away more informed about "the Good Book," and apart from their vital "other-world orientation," they are often better equipped to deal with the harsh realities of life. No offense, but the rock-and-roll groups or the reggae and dub places have not won the battle for enjoyment over these Christians.

The Caribbean is the better for having produced indigenous men of God like evangelist Baldwin. With the wave of decadence, immorality and crass materialism presently sweeping this socio-cultural area, God's church has an even more critical and decisive role as "the salt of the earth," against the background of Maranatha. In keeping with this thinking, the Caribbean religious elite loses sight of the fullness of its mission if and when, even with good intentions, they are like clones of the metropolitan ministers. Even though God is constant, the social psychology of Caribbean people is unique and different and so must be those who address the spiritual needs of its peoples.

VI

RACE AND ETHNIC RELATIONS

Rastas Are People Too

VI Daily News, October 10, 1983: 6.

I WAS APPALLED AND incensed by the contents of your Sept. 27 front-page article which alluded to the fact that non-B.V.I. Rastafarians are barred from visiting the neighboring British Virgin Islands, as exemplified in the recent experience of Leroy Williams, a citizen of Jamaica.

Seemingly, the reason behind this regulation, according to Edmund Maduro, B.V.I. chief immigration officer, hinges on the assumption or rather presumption that Rastas do "not fit into the B.V.I. way of life."

But tell me, what constitutes the B.V.I. way of life? And since when does one segment of the B.V.I. society have the constitutional right and temerity to impose its ethnocentric, myopic concept of what it insularly regards as the B.V.I. way of life on others who may care to visit its shores?

The supposed protection of the B.V.I.'s way of life from what is designated as an alien sub-culture is nothing more than a euphemism for anti-Rasta sentiment and one that is spreading.

But what is frightening and an ironic cause for concern is that such a course of action is strangely reminiscent of the pre-civil rights movement era during which time, Blacks, a conspicuous minority, were denied their civil liberties on the basis of physical appearance and other dubious grounds.

Are democratic-minded Virgin Islanders going to sit idly by and allow history to repeat itself? It is now transparently clear that the denial of non-resident Rasta entry to the B.V.I. is tantamount to an infringement of the civil liberties of the individual and should therefore be identified by its right name i.e., discrimination? Or do B.V.I. authorities have a legitimate and uncontestable right to determine whom they regard as undesirables?

Let it be known that Rastas, as a group, are people too and discrimination against them is discrimination nonetheless. Irrespective of the indefensible wrong-doings perpetrated by some Rastas, as is true of other segments of the society, why are Rastas singled out as the ones to be preyed upon? And why can't Rastas, an admittedly unconventional-looking group, be allowed to travel freely and without harassment by immigration officials, be they B.V.I. or otherwise?

If this discriminatory action goes unchecked, conceivably it could produce a sort of physical-appearance pass-system in the Caribbean, very much like the pass laws in South Africa.

With this in mind, I implore the freedom-loving readers of your daily issue to speak out against this dastard action for fear of the same spreading to the U.S. Virgin Islands and to other parts of the Caribbean where the Rasta way of life is seen as an alternative, however uninviting it may appear to the good gentleman Maduro and others of his persuasion.

Indeed, no man is truly free until all men are free and I dare say, any such freedom, includes freedom to travel, even to the B.V.I.

Trinidad & Tobago Ban on Stokely Carmichael Lifted

Caribbean Contact (Barbados), February 1985: 9.

Stokely Carmichael, now known as Kwame Ture, visited the Virgin Islands late last year. This was expected to be the first of many Caribbean visits since it appears that the government of Trinidad & Tobago has now rescinded Ture's 17-year ban to travel to his native land. He will be permitted to visit close relatives who are seriously ill and have requested to see him.

The Trinidadian-born Californian Congressman Mervyn Dymally, national President of a US-based lobby for the Caribbean, was influential in the Trinidadian government's change of attitude toward Ture. Such a decision came at a time when, in the aftermath of the US-led Grenada invasion, many of the English-speaking Caribbean countries have placed unprecedented emphasis on defense and security and have become increasingly suspicious of figures like Kwame Ture.

Ture gave an address to the College of the Virgin Islands (CVI), the only black land grant institution outside of the continental USA. CVI, the only state-run American institution of higher learning in the English-speaking Caribbean, has recently been declared the home of the Eastern Caribbean Centre, another idea of the Reagan. Administration to address the socio-economic problems of the sub-region.

In his address at the Reichhold Centre for the Arts, Ture told Virgin Islanders: "Disorganization is the major obstacle towards liberation and is a common thread throughout black communities. While Blacks flounder without unity, the enemy is organized at every level." Ture cited "racism, capitalism, neo-colonialism and the people who support these systems" as the enemy.

However, contrary to what might be expected from an avowed socialist, Ture looks askance at African leaders like Mengistu Haile Mariam of Ethiopia, Samora Machel of Mozambique and Jose dos Santos of. Angola, who have aligned their countries with the Soviet Union and adopted 'a socialism' which Ture contends is alien to Africa and Black people everywhere. Unlike Grenada's former Deputy Prime Minister Bernard Coard, he does not see any virtue in European Marxism-Leninism. Such an ideology, says Ture, fails to deal with the 20th century realities of racism and world racial polarization and ignores the fact that socialism has its roots in African communal systems.

Ture, a political activist, author and party organizer, has remained remarkably committed to his vision of sweeping social change. Few move steadily, or remain to the left as they grow older, and so few display that bravery conferred by utter certainty of conviction.

He has not retreated from his advocacy of black power. In contemporary times, his political outlook is based on the twin foundation of Nkrumahism and Pan-Africanism – what Ture designates "the highest political expressions of black power."

Virgin Islands' Students Protest Apartheid

Caribbean Contact (Barbados), November 1985: 9.

ON SATURDAY, OCTOBER 19, 1985, more than 150 marchers from diverse segments of the US Virgin Islands community came together, in spite of the manifest political apathy that plague these lovely islands, to protest the racist policies of the Botha regime in South Africa. Chanting anti-apartheid slogans, many carrying banners and posters, the protesters marched from the Addelita Cancryn Junior High School on the outskirts of the city to the Emancipation Garden in down-town Charlotte Amalie, the capital of St. Thomas, St. Croix and St. John.

The occasion was inspired and organized by the College of the Virgin Islands (CVI) student government, under the leadership of Clement 'Gold' Hodge, a native of Anguilla and the first Rastafarian to become the president of a student government at the College of the Virgin Islands. Among those speakers who made statements on the occasion which lasted for well over two hours were Dr. Charles Turnbull, Commissioner of Education, Dr. Arthur Richards, CVI president, the Honourable Ron DeLugo, a native white and the territory's only representative to the US Congress; other elected officials such as Senators Lorraine Berry and pro-black, controversial Adelbert Bryan, two candidates in the race for governor in the local November 1986 election, as well as black nationalist Mario Moorhead, head of the

United Caribbean Association, a leftist, pro-independence, political pressure group in the Virgin Islands.

There was unified condemnation of President Reagan's policy of "constructive engagement". Several speakers called for stronger economic sanctions, while others pointed to the need to arm South African blacks. Delegate-to-Congress DeLugo stated that his own arrest outside the South African Embassy in Washington, D.C., showed his commitment to the fight against apartheid.

But the ire of the demonstrators was not focused on Pretoria alone. Calypsonian Glenn 'Kwabena' Davis accused local politicians of getting political mileage from the much publicized event while giving a blind eye to local businesses run by 'continentals' (white Americans) who often practice racism at the expense of blacks who reside in the Virgin Islands.

Emotions ran high when demonstrators held hands and sang "We Shall Overcome", the hymn Benjamin Moloise sang on his way to the gallows. CVI professor Gene Emanuel referred to the hanging of Moloise as "cold blooded murder", and called the South African authorities "murderous dogs". Rev. Charles Peters, a Moravian minister, gave his blessing to the violent overthrow of the Pretoria government and echoed: "If Christians are prepared to pray for freedom; they must be prepared to fight for that very freedom."

The spirit of the occasion seemed to strongly suggest that the struggle inside South Africa, although necessary, is not sufficient if apartheid is to be dismantled. Rather, the chilly wind of international disapproval, economic boycotts and disinvestment are necessary if peace and freedom are to be won in South Africa.

---◈---

BLACKS HAVE LONG WAY TO GO
CVI Post, April 9, 1985: 2.

"**FREE AT LAST**, Free at last, thank God Almighty, we are free at last." This refrain of a well-known Negro spiritual was woven into the late Dr. Martin Luther King's celebrated speech at the Washington monument on that unforgettable summer day in 1963.

The social rebellion in the United States was at its peak. Many persons had lost their lives and some were injured amidst racial conflict. The descendants of Slave owners and the enslaved, respectively, were the principal participants in this drama. Dr. King, the descendant of a slave, dreamt of the day when his and subsequent generations would live in racial harmony in the land void of the salient vestiges of slavery. And so, Dr. King, like others before him, spoke of the need for freedom to reign.

The United States might not yet be free of acute racial injustice were it not for the civil rights movement of the 1960s. But out of conflict came social change, and the "social revolution" of that period did much to forge a better understanding and accommodation between the races, however, superficial. Given the prevailing circumstances, such a rebellion was useful. The South now is a better place. The freedom of Blacks is less mangled even here in the Virgin Islands.

Violence is among the expedients of the black revolt. Indeed, it was only one in the arsenal of weapons used. Equally important was the legacy of bondage and the articulation of the problem. The descendants of the enslaved found great orators in such spokespersons as King, Malcolm X, Elizah Mohammed, Bayard Rustin, Angela Davis and Stokely Carmichael, a recent visitor to the College of the Virgin Islands (CVI). Even lesser known Virgin Islander figures like Roy Inniss and Mario Moorhead are part of this landscape. So far reaching and profound were the events of the 1960s that it can be argued with merit that Malcolm X and Martin Luther King, Jr. were to the reformism of the 1960's, what Jean Jacques Rousseau was to the French Revolution of 1789; or Thomas Paine to the "bigger revolution" of 1776.

Yes, the blatant and strident racial injustices that conditioned and kept Black people in their place is a thing of the past in the New World, but are they free as a people. Today, blacks are able to vote; more readily experience upward mobility. And maybe the day is not too far off when a black person will be elected president. But black people are still working through the process of emancipation. There is a spiritual and psychological freedom that still has to be attained in the Virgin Islands and the Caribbean before blacks can truly and honestly say "Free at last, free at last, thank God Almighty, we are free at last."

One way toward genuine freedom is to pursue an understanding of one's history with discernment, and one's education at CVI ought to do precisely that. Knowledge is power. It is the source of freedom. In the Caribbean, the descendants of the enslaved must not only understand, but act out this maxim in their lives.

◆

CALL OPPRESSION BY ITS RIGHT NAME

St. Croix Avis, June 21, 1994: 6; VI
Daily News, June 23, 1994: 16.

B OTH IN AND out of academia, it is not uncommon for scholars, thinkers and others, particularly the Black Nationalist and Pan-Africanists, to contend that a great deal of suffering in the Caribbean region and on the African continent is due to white oppression.

There is no denying that new world slavery, colonialism and apartheid in South Africa were the result of racism that was perpetrated by Europeans. However, this point of view appears to be only one side of the coin.

It is conspicuously noticeable that Black leaders, both on the U.S. mainland and in the Caribbean, including the Virgin Islands, who were quite vociferous about South Africa, appear to be quite silent about genocide taking place in Rwanda. It has been estimated that, over the period of a couple of weeks, upwards of 500,000 people may have been slaughtered on account of this dastardly conflict.

If this is confirmed to be true, this eventuality may well be a human tragedy comparable to none that we have witnessed in recent times.

In Haiti, a country that has the watershed distinction of being the first Black republic but today is the poorest country in the Western Hemisphere, people are being murdered left and right. However, against this backdrop, Caribbean countries are refusing to accept Haitian refugees fleeing political oppression, and the few that have been accepted is a mere sprinkling.

By so doing, these Black nation states, as in the case of Rwanda, appear to be silent and/or pay lip service to human tragedy when it is politically expedient.

Would the responses of Black nationalists, Pan-Africanists and others of like mind, in and out of elected office, be different if Rwandans were being killed by whites and the Haitian masses dominated by the French? Why not call oppression by its right name regardless of its source?

◈

Krigger's Book Sheds New Light
on V.I. Race Relations
VI Daily News, March 24, 2018: 15.

UVI Professor Emerita of History Dr. Marilyn F. Krigger has recently published <u>Race Relations in the U.S. Virgin Islands – St. Thomas: A Centennial Perspective</u>, which is propitious, given the great interest in the topic of race relations in the United States where there are signs of a deepening racial divide. However, that interpretation may be different for the Virgin Islands.

There are different kinds of historians. Those with several degrees in the subject who are usually based at universities; those who research and write outside of academia; and those who are "public historians" whose knowledge about the past can be captured by observing them on social media, talk shows, as well as in the public square. But as long as historians like Professor Krigger translate their ideas to writing, their work will outlive them and become part of the storehouse of knowledge.

Her book explores the evolution of race relations in the U.S. Virgin Islands and is divided into three overarching parts: Part 1: The Danish Foundation, 1672-1917; Part 2: The First Half-Century of the United States Sovereignty, 1917-1967; and Part 3: The Second Half-Century of United States Sovereignty, 1967-2017. These three are further subdivided into 22 chapters, with an extensive bibliography. Methodologically, Krigger employed archival and literature sources and between 1982 and

2017, interviewed or consulted 209 persons which is testimony that this project was a life-long labor of love.

Chapter 19, "Race Relations in Education, 1967-2017," seems dear to the heart of the author, in part because she has been a participant-observer. From the perspective of a former public school teacher at the Charlotte Amalie High School, she does not mince words, noting that "the public school system, in many ways, was both a victim of and a contributor to the new racial configuration…."

The sub-section in that very chapter explores the vagaries and triumphs of the University of the Virgin Islands, which was started in 1963. It is anecdotal, well referenced, and underscores the role of the Territory's only institution of higher learning, serving as an enhancement of the middle class and a buffer of sorts. However, she does mention that "the creation of UVI was one of the greatest events in VI history as it allows poor Blacks to get access to higher education."

It is in chapter 22, entitled "Centennial Thoughts and Prospects" that the author reveals her innermost thoughts. She avers that "the state of race relations in St. Thomas, U.S. Virgin Islands, is far from good" and expresses with anguish that the patrimony of the island's residents seems to be under threat by a kind of gentrification.

"Apparently, St. Thomas, (and other parts of the Virgin Islands and similar places) are now considered by some to be so beautiful and conducive to good living that they should be best utilized by the wealthy, with others going elsewhere to live" she writes.

Researching and writing history is a cumulative process, and it depends on the output of generations of historians whose work build upon that of their predecessors.

The platform on which Dr. Krigger has found herself is a space shared by the following publications: <u>A Christian Mission </u>by G. A. Oldendorp (1777); <u>A History of the Virgin Islands of the United States</u> by Isaac Dookhan (1974); <u>America's Virgin Islands: A History of Human Rights</u>

and Wrongs by William Boyer (1983); The Umbilical Cord: The History of the United States Virgin Islands from the Pre-Columbian Era to the Present by Harold W. L. Willocks (1995); and many others including the works of Drs. Arnold Highfield, Aimery Caron, Charles Turnbull, the deceased Jamaican Neville Hall, Ruth Moolenar and Eddie Donaghue. These authors have made significant contributions to the writings of V.I. history and hence have added to the corpus of knowledge about the territory.

However, Dr. Krigger's book, with an emphasis on race relations, is groundbreaking. It is the first on race relations in the Virgin Islands by "a black native and resident of the Virgin Islands" and hence fills the lacuna that has long existed.

The author's selection of the topic was influenced by her admiration for President Abraham Lincoln who passed the laws that freed the American slaves, along with her harrowing experience of being ejected from her seat and gruffly directed to the back of the bus when a student at Spelman College in Atlanta, contrary to the accustomed practice in her native St. Thomas, America's paradise. Notwithstanding, the seeds of this publication are very likely traceable to the impact of the late Mrs. Mary Skelton Francis, Charlotte Amalie High social science teacher and Dr. Krigger's mother, confidante, and mentor, to whose memory the book is dedicated, plus the impact of her husband, Rudolph E. Krigger, and three special CVI/UVI alumni: Raymond Joseph, Dana Orie and Valentine Penha.

Their support allowed the author to join the list of Caribbean scholars who have published books on race relations in the Caribbean. These include pioneers whose work laid the foundations for others to follow, namely, Eric Williams' The Negro in the West Indies (1942); Raymond T. Smith's, Race and Class in Post-Emancipation Caribbean (1956) and M.G. Smith's, The Plural Society in the Caribbean (1965).

This book contributes greatly to the charting of a new and more enlightened path within the field of race relations and for that reason should be studied closely by all students of the New World historical experience.

VII

HIGHER EDUCATION

The University of the Virgin Islands Needs More Resources

VI Daily News, March 19, 1987: 6.

T<small>HIS YEAR MARKS</small> the 25th birthday of our beloved University of the Virgin Islands (UVI). It is a time of rejoicing, and the celebrations this week should evoke a feeling of pride.

It also is a time for reflection as UVI faces the challenges of the future, part and parcel of which is the consummation of its transition from a college to a full-fledged university.

What does it mean to be a university? Unthinking people may brush aside this query. Nevertheless, there is significance of substance in a name when chosen. A name brings with it certain attributes and qualities that ought to be borne out.

In its comparatively short existence, UVI can boast of offering baccalaureate degrees in business administration, humanities, nursing, science and mathematics, social sciences and education, as well as master's degrees in education, business administration and public administration.

These offerings, along with its impressive Reichhold Center for the Arts, are commendable, with the latter contributing immeasurably to the cultural ethos of the territory.

The metamorphosis is enough to demonstrate to the Legislature, to other powers that be, and even to its critics, what UVI has done. It should also remind us that we cannot afford to jeopardize its existence and hinder it from functioning as an institution of the highest quality. However, the change of name is cause for pause.

There is more to a university than meets the eye. I will concern myself with one fundamental feature: scientific inquiry. It is a major, not minor, role of a university, and some colleges too, to foster the institutionalization of research. This serves to demonstrate to the world outside the university that its work is not limited to lectures given to students.

Teaching and research are common bedfellows, as has indeed been the case in the U.S. institutions of higher learning since the arrival of the German influence a century ago. Such activities are not like parallel lines; rather each informs and enhances the other.

Beyond the regular emolument, a university professor is rarely rewarded for what he or she knows. Along with other considerations, merit is bestowed for the new facts and theories one brings home to the "intellectual tribe." This feature distinguishes a university from a public high school.

Pursuant to this, if this recent name change is to have credence and resonate as a new genesis, as presumably it must, business as usual ought not to prevail. For a university to be true to itself and its mission, as reflected in its designation, it is incumbent that it not only be a place where tertiary knowledge is found, reflected upon and transmitted, but also that research must be a central element of the work there.

In brief, without abdicating its pre-eminent task of teaching, it is expected that a university will create knowledge. UVI's Caribbean Research Institute, begun in 1964, is a fitting acknowledgement of this principle and undoubtedly was created to this end. This body has the makings of becoming a "think tank" to address more forthrightly some of the near-intractable problems which currently face the territory, as echoed in the inaugural addresses by Gov. Alexander Farrelly, and Lt. Gov. Derek Hodge.

UVI's reaffirmation of its role to coincide with its silver anniversary, together with its decided name change, is a watershed in its history. But those reasons which justify a change of name without a change in the academic offerings, scope and texture of the educational process or a promise of same, are beyond my ken.

The University has tremendous and unimaginable potential, and its next five years will quite possibly be the most pivotal and critical in its history.

It is hoped, with the greatest of respect, that if and when incumbent President Arthur Richards steps down from the helm, the election of his successor, who will likely take the university into the 21st century, will not be cursory and predicated on parochial grounds, but that an individual with vision and some "public relations flare" will be earmarked for the job. Future Board of Trustees conferees should be appointed with no less haste and care.

Present and future UVI administrations are hamstrung if additional funding for the operation of the university, including its library, is not commensurate with the tasks of that lies ahead. Conceivably, Gov. Alexander Farrelly and the present Legislature who, with alacrity, are inclined to hike their salaries on the rationale that you get what you pay for, hopefully will not be hard to convince.

If UVI is to build on its strengths and maximize the true meaning of its recently adopted name, this actuality will require a greater commitment of resources, not only for the research endeavor, but for the overall program of the university.

UVI Battles back from Hugo

VI Daily News, October 19, 1990: 10.

T HE 27-YEAR-OLD UNIVERSITY of the Virgin Islands, with campuses in St. Thomas and St. Croix, as well as an ecological research station in St. John, has over the years faced many crises. But none compares in magnitude with the dislocation that Hurricane Hugo has wrought.

Classes have had to be disbanded for a period in excess of a month, with a tentative startup date of Oct. 23. The reconstruction effort mounted by the university in the wake of this "act of God" is a test of the mettle of its leadership cadre. This is similarly the case with the political directorate, commissioners and others in the larger body politic.

The 1989-90 academic year at UVI, the last for the retiring president Arthur Richards, was in its second month with an enlarged student enrollment of 2,665. Also, the territory's only state-run institution of higher learning, like the public sector at the behest of the Farrelly administration, has undergone restructuring that resulted in an expanded compliment of six vice presidents, a change that some contend is oblivious to any possibility of a natural disaster, since none is a maintenance technocrat.

As is customary, UVI's physical plant department took the necessary precautions as the hurricane approached, which included protection of some of the many campus buildings. However, when Hugo hit with its devastating force, it wreaked havoc on both campuses, more so in St. Croix, in much the same fashion that it did in Guadeloupe, Montserrat, Puerto Rico, St. Kitts-Nevis and other Eastern Caribbean islands.

The scene on both campuses on the morning of Sept. 18, the day after the hurricane, was awesome and unbelievable, especially to those of us who have come to know and love the special beauty of this citadel of learning. Numerous trees, some of which were regular fixtures on both campuses, were uprooted and brought low in the fury of Hurricane Hugo. So turbulent were the tornado-type winds that the catchment on the St. Thomas campus, which forms a backdrop to the golf course as you pass by the roadway intersecting the campus, was pitted by gaping holes.

Amidst the damage to UVI's dormitory facilities, where 258 students reside, none of them suffered any injury and as is true of the general outcome of Hurricane Hugo, it remains a mystery that so few lives were lost.

On UVI's main campus on St. Thomas, three buildings were hard hit. Continuing Education, Teacher Education and the Ralph M. Paiewonsky Library, which houses the offices of top administrators, including the president, and the library proper, all of which are on the "upper campus."

Undoubtedly, along with other critical factors, the inability to continue optimum library service may have featured prominently in the decision to temporarily close.

Many other buildings on the St. Thomas campus suffered damage, but none as grave as the Harvey Student Center that contains, among other things, the cafeteria, which was decimated.

The Social Sciences and similar buildings that dot the St. Thomas campus – former residences of Navy officers, seemingly constructed to withstand the ravages of World War II – apart from sporadic leaking roofs, generally stood up well. With this in mind, a survey should be conducted throughout the Virgin Islands to identify which building systems are best suited to withstand hostile weather.

The Reichhold Center, where artistic talent is often demonstrated, was, by comparison, unscathed. With the restoration of power, it appears that the major productions and other events can be accommodated as soon as the community is ready for such cultural embellishments.

As is the general pattern, the destruction to the St. Croix campus dwarfs that of St. Thomas. To the casual observer, there may appear to be minimal damage to the cluster of buildings called the Melvin Evans Learning Center, which includes the library. However, the truth is that internal damage is extensive and stunning. The mutilated condition of the Agricultural Service speaks for itself, and so the story goes.

It will be awhile before the full extent of the damage to the university is ascertained. Until such time, what seems to be certain is that the institution, already strapped financially – as evidenced by the carefully orchestrated demonstration at the Legislature last year for increased fiscal support – has been dealt what is perhaps not a moral blow, but certainly a crippling injury.

The university-wide recovery efforts on both campuses are appropriately spearheaded by President Richards. The ensuing plans that have been devised to ameliorate the pressing problems require that, where possible, university employees put shoulder to the wheel. This is no time for good people to do nothing.

As is often the case, in the politics of crisis-management, there are signs of jockeying for power among "the president's men" who, together with the broader coordinated strategy, will in due course, put UVI back on track.

Without a doubt, the recovery drive to regain normalcy for UVI is expected to underscore the resiliency, not only of the university community, but the people of the Virgin Islands in general.

Women Play Key Roles at UVI
VI Daily News, October 24, 2011: 22.

P ERHAPS WOMEN NO longer can cry exploitation or bemoan inequality and the lack of opportunity compared with men in the workplace and other arenas. Perhaps the system no longer can be alleged to favor men over women.

In contemporary times, across the United States, women are assuming leading roles in higher education. The University of the Virgin Islands has always been a leader in this. As a striking example of this trend, Shirley Lake-King recently became UVI's first female Vice President of Administration and Finance.

It would be a misconception to construe Lake-Kings's elevation to this cherished and coveted position, at the right hand of the male university president, Dr. David Hall, as necessarily and entirely a politically correct concession to the feminist impulse.

It appears that Shirley Lake-King's greatest strengths, which have allowed her to circumvent the glass ceiling, if one exist at UVI, reside in her professional competence and a solid value system, which invites trust and security as a team player in the work place. Her strength of character should equip her to make sterling contributions to the presidential team as the university holds its own in these trying times.

Shirley Lake-King seems to be another demonstration of the heights to which competent women can climb. UVI's last president, LaVerne Ragster, the fourth UVI president, left her mark on the institution. The appointment of Lake-King may well serve as an inspiration and positive example for others to follow. She is aware that "to whom much is given, much is expected."

VIII

SOCIAL ISSUES

❧❧❧

Juvenile Delinquency Is Spiraling

VI Daily News, July 12, 2006: 20.

MORE AND MORE adolescents and young adults are increasingly falling prey to crime or delinquency. Whereas a crime is an act that breaks the law, delinquency and deviance can be acts that merely break society's norms. Delinquency is usually specific and tied to the age of the perpetrator.

In the Virgin Islands, the rest of the Caribbean and the world at large, juvenile delinquency is a big and growing problem. Correction facilities multiply with juvenile offenders, mostly males, who have been convicted of various crimes. As a result of incarceration, rehabilitation, if and when it does exist, is proving to be a costly proposition for governments in an era of financial stringency.

If a person associates with more groups that define criminal behavior as acceptable rather than groups that define criminal behavior as unacceptable, the person will probably be more susceptible to criminal behavior. Though this theory does not explain how some individuals who are surrounded by criminality resist opportunities to engage in criminal behavior, it is felt that deviance, like conforming behavior, is a product of socialization.

Parents and peers are probably the most powerful agents of socialization. To exemplify this theory, imagine a child growing up in a home where the parents routinely engage in criminal acts. More often than not, the child will grow up assuming that these acts may not be wrong as society or the law defines them.

Also, if a child consort with delinquents, he or she can learn the activities of its peers and be much more prone to engage in criminal behavior. Hence, it behooves parents to consistently set the right example and to monitor their children's friends to stymie and avert possible delinquent behavior.

The rational choice theory on the other hand is proffered by those who view juvenile delinquency from an individual-based perspective. There are some psychologists who contend that those who deviate sometimes do not fully know what they are doing. Here, crime is a way to express certain irresistible pathological urges. They may be influenced by the anxiety caused by maternal deprivation, low moral development or a defective conscience that is perhaps so weak that the individual is unable to control the unconscious impulses.

Would-be deviants choose to commit crimes after weighing their chances of gain against the risks of getting caught and thereby decide upon a course of action. In others words, individuals have free-will to choose legal or illegal means to get what they want. Hence society, and by extension the criminal justice systems, can control criminal behavior by making the pain of punishment greater than the pleasure of criminal gain.

However, juveniles do not always pursue the most rational courses of action. Often their values and goals are different from those of adults and at times the mainstream culture. In fact, some adolescents are notorious for not thinking before they act. However, some aspire to a so-called middle class lifestyle, which may include academic achievement and the accoutrements of life. When these aspirations are not realized, they seek self-esteem by rejecting those values and substituting their own.

This rejection is often impulsive – without weighing and considering the consequences – pleasure-seeking, malicious and non-utilitarian. This explains why on occasion some youth are wanton – they delight in the discomfort of others and may not sell for profit, but destroy the things they steal.

Sometimes, this bizarre behavior is a result of acting out against authority or rebelling against cultural norms and goals. For example, a juvenile may decide to ignore school rules; randomly set off a smoke alarm; destroy property, including computers, as an act of defiance toward administrative authority in a learning institution. In these circumstances "partners to the crime" often act autonomously and are so loyal to one another that they resist any attempt to restrain or divulge their behavior not only to police investigators but their own families and all others in the community. In this milieu, the fad of tainted auto windows can add to the cover of darkness that surrounds dastard acts. In jurisdictions where this is allowed, in the name of freedom, governments may be guilty of unwitting complicity to offences that could have otherwise been avoided, not to mention their obvious hindrance to the apprehension of offenders by law enforcement officials.

It is therefore incumbent on everyone, particularly parents, to be a positive controlling force in the life of young people, particularly their own children, by setting the right example. Whether we are aware or not, there is always someone who may be emulating us, most of all our own children. If indeed it takes "a village to raise a child."

Almost all adults are surrogate parents and our responsible behavior can contribute, however infinitesimally, to the decline of delinquency and positively impact socioeconomic development as well as enhance the quality of life.

$\diamondsuit$

REFLECTIONS ON SUICIDE

St. Croix Avis, April 1, 1997: 3; VI
Daily News, April 3, 1997: 12.

S UICIDE IS DISTURBING. Each time human beings commit this act of finality, whether individually or collectively, the latter exemplified by 39 members of Heaven's Gate in Rancho Santé Fe, California on March 26, 1997, the compelling question with which we are faced is "why?"

To the family or families of the suicide victims, the pain of that "why" is intensely personal and haunting. To the wider society, the hurt is dissipated by its distance from the tragedy and the "why" is often asked in generalities.

There is no model to provide information to families, professionals and the public at large on suicide causation and prevention. It is difficult to assimilate all the basic information and conclude that one or more factors contribute to suicide. However, some of the reasons theorized by researchers for committing suicide are aggression turned inward, efforts to rid oneself of unacceptable feelings, and attempts to make amends for perceived past wrongs.

In some instances, individuals commit suicide because there is a strong desire for reincarnation (rebirth of the soul in a new body) or the desire to join a loved one. Often, individuals engage in this ultimate act to escape from stressful situations and when feelings of depression pervade the entire emotional system.

When suicide notes are taken into consideration, it has been found that such notes are full of compassion, affection and appear to be contrary to notions of "hostility directed inward." However, one must consider that these notes are often written with the intent to appear rational and passive. In other words, they are written at a conscious level and hence suppress feelings of depression, hostility and aggression, all or some of which pertain. People can so cloth their depression in a façade of well-being, coolness or intellectualism, so much so that when the worst happens, those who are close to them are the most shocked.

Although the act of killing oneself appears to be self-inflicting, Emile Durkheim, a French sociologist, has long felt that it is essentially a social act. Back in 1897, he indicated that there were three kinds of suicide across cultures.

The first is egoistic suicide. This is committed when the individual is not integrated into or involved with groups such as the family, church and/or community. In other words, individuals do not see their behavior as having any consequence for some meaningful group.

The second is anomic suicide. This occurs in situations of confusion or contradiction when there are no stable norms that guide and regulate one's behavior. In present day post-modern society, which is characterized by relativism, rapid change, hastened by the computer chip, and void of absolutes that often give meaning to life, the immaculate living environment of Sante Fe cult members shown to viewers of CNN news is conspicuous. This may well be part of the group's quest for order on this side of the great divide, the other side being "Heaven," ushered in by the Hale-Bopp comet, which appears to be focal to the group's eschatology.

The third is altruistic suicide which occurs when the individual places the furtherance of the group's ideals and goals ahead of his or her own life. In other words, the identity of the individual becomes so intertwined with the goals and survival of the group that the latter takes precedence. Hence, at the bidding of the group's leader, ostensibly charismatic, group members find it difficult to separate what is good for the individual from that of the group. The peer pressure mentality takes root in the collective consciousness that if we all die, I cannot be left out – more so, if the reason for dying is internalized as a thing of value. Reality is not inherent in the thing itself, but in its social construction.

The case of the 913 persons, led by Jim Jones, who committed mass suicide in Jonestown, Guyana, in 1978 and the 39 in Santa Fe led by Marshall "Dow" Applewhite, appear to be two examples of both anomic and altruistic suicide.

Though useful, Durkheim's typology is limited in that it does not explain why one person will commit suicide when faced with the moment of truth while another will opt out of the circumstance. This is still an unknown for the Santa Fe incident but in the Jonestown scenario, those who attempted to take flight were shot on sight.

There are various symptoms of imminent suicide. Persons processing suicidal behavior may break off social ties, give away prized possessions, sleep excessively, decrease or increase eating habits or refuse to carry out routine activities, such as attendance at work, school or engaging in regular household chores. It should also be noted that would-be suicides tend to be very rigid in their thinking and also think in extremes.

As individuals and as a society, it behooves us to be more perceptive and responsive to the behavior of others as a way of reducing and preventing suicide. A lot will depend on close friends and relatives becoming alert to the danger signs and not allow people who are so prone to become victims to such desperate action.

--- ◈ ---

Rapid Changes in Our Society
May Be Causing More Crime

VI Daily News, March 4, 1988: 10.

C RIME IN THE U.S. Virgin Islands is attracting quite a bit of attention these days. The print media, radio and television, the Legislature, residents of the territory, particularly those that are affected – even the police force itself – all display concern at what is touted as the sudden rise in criminality.

It is not only offenses against property, some of which involve unlawful entry, but violent crimes like those that transpired during Carnival '87 and the bloody attack on Rabbi Stanley Relkin that evoke some measure of anxiety in all of us. Who will be next?

On Good Morning America, Gov. Alexander Farrelly spoke of the increase in crime as part and parcel of the prevailing development thrust. This may be so, but if the current trend persists, residents will likely, at their own expense, purchase more insurance against burglary, acquire safes and watchdogs and install burglary bars.

There are psychic disadvantages as well. According to Relkin's Feb. 11 <u>Daily News</u> guest editorial, "Walking in our main business area or attending worship services at our major religious institutions is dangerous."

Seemingly, many people nowadays often are scared to leave their homes. This is a sad omen because people who feel threatened are inclined to procure firearms, either legally or illegally. Also, the demand for heavier punishment becomes stronger. In short, the community we like to think of as a paradise runs the risk of becoming a rather grim place.

Criminality may be defined as lawbreaking conduct. The offenses against property and person, many of which are carried out by Blacks, are but a part thereof. Deliberately filling out income tax returns incorrectly, accepting bribes, embezzlement, fraud, malfeasance, these are all frequently occurring phenomena that can just as well be called crime, and which unfortunately cause as much or even more damage to the community than the offenses that are getting so much attention at the moment.

But one can hardly perceive any alarm on that account. Conceivably, the existing opinion about this form of criminality seems to suggest that it is not as morally censurable, and only reprehensive when the offenders, who typically operate beyond the long arm of the law, are caught. However, in our focus on crime and its prevention, we are derelict if and when we exclude the white-collar kind.

Respect for normal authority in today's Virgin Islands is at a low ebb. The pattern is undesirable. However, we fool ourselves if we conceive of this as new. Buccaneering, privateering, smuggling, the legal exploitation of a human being by another through slavery –which existed here until 1848 – and also profiteers from wars elsewhere, have been important sources of income and are, undeniably, part of our heritage, or at least to the extent that we are a pluralistic society.

Actually, even in contemporary times, our society, in many ways, still operates on the edge of the law. The current economy is replete with activities, like offshore banking, that examples have shown cannot bear too much exposure. No wonder we have so far stayed clear of the casino business.

What is particularly noticeable about the current wave of crime is the high incidence of violent crime. Cruzan clinical psychologist Copeland goes so far as to dub this behavior as reminiscent of prerevolutionary activity.

The rapid social and economic changes have brought progress to many, black and white alike. It cannot be gainsaid that locals sit in the Legislature and hold other key positions.

However, because of the influx of continentals and others, as well as the heavy penetration of U.S. mainland culture, more and more "*born here*" and "*belong here*" do not feel that they are being treated justly in such areas as job procurement, housing and property acquisition and that the integrity of the local culture is not always given due respect. There is intense pressure on the "local population."

Many residents, particularly our youth, even the native middle class, are confused or befuddled as to what is really happening to them. One such response to this frustration is evidenced by Virgin Islands 2000, the existence of which implies an attempt to restore a way of life that is being threatened. However, this very frustration can also, and may be, provoking violent acts.

Often, people react with force when they are, or perceive themselves to be, pushed around even within the legal frame. Here, criminal behavior has a significant function. It smacks of a refusal, on the part of some, to accept things as they are. It is a sign that certain groups expect so little of our social order that they place themselves outside this order and reject its values.

Crime in the Virgin Islands is extremely complex. An increase in expenditures for law enforcement will help, but it is not likely to have a significant effect. The causes of criminality are rooted in the very fabric of our society and culture and long-term strategies at prevention are obliged to take such into consideration.

◈

LEGALIZING MARIJUANA FOR MEDICAL USE

St. Croix Avis, November 21, 2014: 14.

M ARIJUANA HAS MEANT so many things to people over the years that it is difficult to describe it from a single perspective. Along with alcohol, it is the most dominant drug in the United States.

So unique, it is not easy to place marijuana within a single classification. Though a psychoactive drug, it is not generally regarded as a stimulant, though it does produce some excitable effect. It is not a hallucinogen, though it can be in large doses. There is no risk of slipping into a coma with marijuana like alcohol. Mostly, it is a highly politicized drug whose advocates carry opposing views.

The first report of its medical usefulness was by Shen Nung in 2737 BC. In AD 2900, Hoatho, another Chinese physician, recommended cannabis resin, mixed with wine, as a surgical anesthetic. Cannabis preparations were used extensively in medicine in India. Almost nothing about cannabis appeared in European medical journals until the 1800s. However, early reports in Europe cite preparations made with cannabis by de Sacy and awakened more interest among writers and artists of the time than the physicians.

In 1860, the Ohio State Medical Society reported the successful use of cannabis in the treatment of stomach pain, chronic cough and gonorrhea. Even though the medical benefits of marijuana have been noted for thousands of years, strong anti-marijuana sentiments in the

U.S. made it difficult until 1970s to conduct an objective appraisal of its clinical applications. Early research in the effectiveness of marijuana to reduce intraocular pressure and dilate bronchioles in the lungs suggested uses as a possible therapy for glaucoma and asthma. However, new prescription medications were shown to be as effective as marijuana in the treatment of these two disorders. In 1985, the FDA licenses a small drug company, Unimed Inc. to begin producing a capsule containing THC for sale to cancer chemotherapy patients who are experiencing nausea. This drug, referred to by the generic name dronabinol (brand name Marinol), has helped cancer chemotherapy patients gain weight, and in 1993, the FDA also approved its use for stimulating appetite in AIDS patients.

Federal officials have resisted the reclassification of marijuana from the Schedule 1 category of controlled substances (drugs that have no medical application) to the Schedule II (which include morphine and cocaine).

Despite opposition from federal officials, advocacy of the medical application of marijuana has grown considerably. With the Territory of the US Virgin Islands on the verge of doing so, some 20 states in the union and the District of Columbia have passed legislature recognizing the use of marijuana for medical purposes, thus allowing patients to use marijuana with physician recommendation or prescription.

The reason for this trend is that proponents of medical marijuana have shown that it is a relatively safe and effective medicine for patients suffering from certain sicknesses and chronic conditions. Of course, opponents contend that medical marijuana is just an excuse for those who want to grow and use the illegal substance.

Without altering its official stance – marijuana is a controlled substance without medical use – the federal government has indicated it will not be a priority of its Justice Department "to use federal resources to prosecute patients with serious medical illnesses or their caregivers who are complying with state law."

However, it has signaled the requirement that the states and territories set up regulations limiting marijuana use to legitimate and medical circumstances; and that it "will not tolerate drug traffickers who hide behind claims of compliance with state law to mask activities that are clearly illegal."

Previously the rejected stone by the political elites, marijuana is now seen, at a time of economic downturn, as potentially part of the corner stone of Caribbean economies, along with tourism and financial services. Legal drug sales and services that generate much-needed revenues could be taxed. However, even though short-term use of marijuana appears to be suitable and effective for treating specific conditions – AIDS, cancer and other serious illnesses – when patients fail to respond to traditional medication, do we really know what are the long-term potential health risks of marijuana? In comparing marijuana to tobacco, it took doctors over 50 years to realize that smoking cigarettes led to lung cancer.

Along with its strengths, it is yet to be determined if marijuana is a two-edged sword. Only time will unravel the truth.

--- ◆ ---

Healthy Marriages Are
Worth the Work

VI Daily News, September 6, 2006: 26.

Today, one out of every two marriages end in divorce. Even among Christians, the anecdotal evidence seems to indicate that the divorce rate inside the church is about the same as it is outside of the church.

Why is it on the rise both in and outside of the church?

Usually, it is not a major life event like infidelity that unhinges the for-better-or-for-worse bond, but rather a string of everyday instances of carelessness and disrespect. Most families in the Caribbean are single-parent females raising their child(ren) outside the context of Christian marriage. However, for couples who court and decide to get married, it is usually on the premise that the institution will bring them the same companionship they experienced during courtship. But for far too many, the enthusiasm fades and then comes alienation, separation and ultimately divorce.

Two distinctions between most Christian and non-Christian are that marriage is for procreation and lifelong companionship – "who therefore God have joined together, let no man put asunder." And so, why is the quality of marital life and divorce among church-goers mirroring that in the mainstream society? Surprisingly, the issues which are driving couples in the church apart are no different from those affecting others who have not committed themselves to a religious way of life.

Whether Christians or not, how does one know that one's marriage is on shaky ground and possibly heading for trouble (if not on the rocks) or still on the road to living happily-ever-after?

Breakdown in communication is the number one marital problem. Effective communication may be sabotaged by using harsh or "gunpowder words," not listening to suggestions and constructive criticism, a partner's tone of voice, nagging and even talking too much, including to receptive in-laws. Self-disclosure is inherent in good communication and is vital in a well-adjusted marriage.

Couples who discuss the day's events as well as the current issues and do something active and cultural on the weekends solidify the marital bond. This could even take the form of church attendance. There may still be some residual truth in the old adage: "The family that prays together, stays together."

Another problem that lends itself to divorce is that the marriage is often not the top priority. Couples should not allow the job and other plausible activities to infringe. They should spend time together, possibly having dinner a few times a week, either at home or a restaurant to spice up the thing. Also, couples should do special things for each other such as buy a little gift or cook a favorite meal. Remembering to acknowledge and celebrate a spouse's birthday and most of all the wedding anniversary are excellent ways to boost a relationship.

Endeavoring to engage in activities that remind each other of the reason for getting married in the first place will also serve to cement the relationship.

Often, the physical attraction and the need to have sex that drew couples together in the beginning can wane. And though romance alone cannot hold a marriage together, touching and kissing in a relationship should not be significantly different from when the couple first met. The age of a marriage does not have to dampen or diminish its romantic life, with or without Viagra. The longevity of the union depends on the continuous display of affection.

Still another cause of "breakup" among couples is that often the two people are in love with themselves. Things never dreamed of as possible in a marriage can occur when both husband and wife are willing to sacrifice selfish interest for the other's joy.

The final reason for divorce is inexperience in conflict resolution. When difficulties arise, including arguments about money management, and they do in the best of marriages, couples should try to expeditiously resolve that which is being fought over and that serves to divide. They should pledge to work through their difficulties until they are effectively communicating and have arrived at problem-solving.

Couples can nip marital stress in the bud if they are aware that it's happening. When a couple's own uninformed attempt at problem-solving seems not to work, it is never too late to seek professional help, including counseling, to resolve marital conflict. On account of the machismo of Caribbean and other men, they find counseling repulsive, but it may be the only thing to salvage a marriage. Paying attention and correcting the course whenever the going gets tough will likely result in a happy, long-term marriage. For there is no success like success in marriage.

Although cultivating healthy marriages and by so doing averting separation and divorce can be hard work, the task produces many delights and great joy. Healthy marriages, not divorces, make the world go on in positive and hopeful ways and may be society's greatest resource.

Are Dishonesty and Corruption in Government Acceptable?

VI Daily News, November 24, 2018: 19.

Honesty is viewed by some as part and parcel of Caribbean societies. Detractors disagree, claiming this is selective reporting and a way to romanticize the past.

The Greek philosopher Diogenes was once seen walking through the streets of Athens carrying a lamp in broad daylight. When asked what he was doing, he replied, "I am looking for an honest man."

Honesty is the value that defines the sanctity of commitments and obligations in contractual and personal relations. Whatever we agree upon, we only make promises and commitments that we are capable of doing; anything we cannot do, we withhold our stake in it. For example, when one becomes the head or leader, they never assign a member of their family or any other relative to work along since this is nepotism.

In contemporary times, honesty seems to be receding. Probably because of the pervasive and insidious effects of materialism, individualism and accompanying greed. We only put a premium on honesty theoretically.

In reality, being honest is relegated to the background. Our excessive desire to own more wealth as well as acquire and retain power – the root causes of the motivation to commit corrupt acts - is so overwhelming that such a virtue seems to be diminishing.

One thing that most people have in common is that we do not like dishonesty. We especially do not like to see it manifested in others, especially government officials, who are meant to be public servants. We are quick to point fingers and it is not easy to see it in ourselves.

The issue of corruption – the misuse of public funds by government officials for they own financial benefit, or the stealing of money provided by taxes that the people pay - dominates the popular media as well as everyday discussions.

The most familiar forms of dishonesty are unethical behavior as well as the political and bureaucratic corruption often attributed to the competitive political system. A form of unethical behavior - and the cousin of corruption - is patronage or the government's preferential gifts. Patronage is not clear-cut criminal activity. Its relationship to corruption lies in the fact that it often wastes the tax payers' money when, for example, contracts go to undeserving friends and supporters. It is used to reward loyalty to the party or politician whose continued support is considered important.

It is quite plausible that in the Caribbean, political competition promotes political and bureaucratic corruption. On the other hand, it may be equally plausible that the region's aggressive competition between candidates and/or parties may be caused by - rather than the cause of - systematic corruption. We cannot accept or deny either proposition because the existing research has not addressed, other than by way of assertion or anecdote, what may be the unique feature of Caribbean governmental systems.

Transparency International (TI), headquartered in Germany, is an international watchdog and its vision is for a world that is free of corruption. TI's Corruption Perceptions Index is part of an annual survey that was started in 1995. Though considered the dominant instrument for measuring corruption, TI does not assert that its instrument is strictly a measure of corruption but merely the perception. However, TI encourages the proposition that if corruption is perceived and it is almost universally assumed, then the index actually measures corruption.

Civil societies across the globe, including those in the Caribbean, are without a reliable measurement at a time when both political and bureaucratic types of corruptions have remained a matter of concern. In fact, corruption has become one of the principal contested issues in Caribbean elections.

It is plausible that there is a causal connection between allegations of corruption against a government and its subsequent performance at the polls. Some governments, as well as candidates who seek office, have campaigned on the promise of fighting corruption. But after assuming office, corruption is often no longer high on the agenda.

This has led to the cynical view that the political elites as a category, present and prospective, use corruption as a campaign ploy, but in their post-election behavior take turns in maladministration, examples of which are graft and corruption.

In 2002, US Secretary of Defense Donald Rumsfeld said, "There are known knows; there are things we know we know. We also know there are known unknowns; that is to say, we know that there are some things we do not know. But there are also unknown unknowns; the ones we don't know we don't know."

Some forms of corruption are clandestine and often times never come to light; *the unknown unknown.* There are corrupt politicians who have cunningly managed to stay on the right side of the law. The criminal justice system is unaware of their nefarious acts. In the case of the United States Virgin Islands, the Justice Department's Public Integrity Section and the Inspector General's Office are left in the dark.

Some forms of corruption are *known unknowns*; they are known by these entities but cannot be substantiated. Corruption has a very high standard of quid pro quo or burden of proof to be established by a prosecutor. Also, someone who accuses another without evidence may be guilty of calumny as well as slander.

Even when high-ranking officials and those in the rank-and-file of government are known to be perpetrators of corruption, far too often, it is the former who can easily get away from being prosecuted because of their influence and power.

Conversely, it is the latter, the so-called "small-fish or low hanging fruit" who usually end up being prosecuted. The dispensation of justice often shows the inequality between two categories – the dominant and the subordinate – and the double system of justice.

Honesty cannot be created by legislative fiat but rather resides in the heart of the individual. It is to be exercised according to an individual's own free-will and conscience. At the same time, there is a need for an injunction, if only to attempt to deter those who might be so inclined to engage in corrupt practices.

One legislative initiative in support of transparency in government has been the introduction of the obligation of public servants to declare their assets in hopes of suppressing corruption. Such assets are put in a blind trust to be administered by an independent trustee. The beneficiary retains absolutely no control over the trust assets during its subsistence. In some jurisdictions, there is a time bar of five years after the date on which the declarant ceases to be a specified person in public life.

Another provision to deter corruption is the enactment of civil forfeiture legislation against those who have gained assets through illegal means. When a person who is, or was, a public official is suspected to be in possession of property or a pecuniary resource that is disproportionate, this enables the state to seize property that is reasonably believed to have been acquired with the proceeds of criminal activity.

Failure to produce evidence to prove that the possession of the property or pecuniary resource was acquired by lawful means may show guilt of an offense and is liable, on summary conviction, to a fine and to imprisonment.

Robust campaign finance reform in elections is another way to tackle corruption. Ideally, in a representative system of governance, the voters choose those that are elected. However, the voice of the voters can be stymied when candidates accept contributions from political and financial interests that have undue influence. Many contributors don't visibly join the campaigning but their behind-the-scenes money amounts to the taking of bribes, which are laundered, in return for extending concessions to benefit donors.

The specter of corruption looms large in the partisan political sphere. As any viewer of the profuse advertisements during political campaigns can attest, the accusation of corruption directed toward one's opponent is increasingly seen as a potent weapon in the rivalry to win an election.

However, when sitting governments shy away from supporting legislative initiatives that are intended to deter corruption, such as the mandatory declaration of assets, civil forfeiture and campaign finance reform - the anticorruption housecleaning that is promised during the heat of the election - it shows the self-serving lip service that is given to the pervasive and corroding issue of corruption.

Caribbean people have historically tended to be tolerant of corrupt politicians and other public servants. Some even excuse it. He or she steals but "get things done." One convicted perpetrator, wishing for exoneration from his actions before sentencing, averred: "I have done a lot of good."

Notwithstanding the nonchalant approach to corruption, the Caribbean, including the Virgin Islands, needs three ingredients to curb corruption and maximize honesty in government. These are

- a stronger legal framework – anti-corruption laws that are implemented.
- committed leaders who stand up for probity, and
- popular mobilization against corruption (This is the most difficult to obtain).

IX

FIRE AND HURRICANES

◆

LESSONS FROM HUGO

St. Croix Avis, October 31, 1989: 12 and 22.

D ISASTERS, AS WAS Hurricane Hugo, are an integral part of human history, although they seem to affect some areas more than others.

The penultimate disaster to be witnessed in the U.S. Virgin Islands was the St. Croix Fountain Valley killings in 1972. Three years prior to that, there was the fatal crash of an American Airline aircraft at the St. Thomas airport. Both of these incidents, though confined to small areas, did extensive damage to the tourist industry. However, neither left widespread desolation, disruption to social organization and wanton grief in their wake as did Hugo.

Unwelcome as it was, Hugo has taught us a great deal about ourselves as a three-island territory. As I rove, I seem to hear untold stories of heroism.

Some heroes and heroines, who are equally deserving of commendation, are members of the VI Police, National Guard and VITEMA, whose efforts, though far from flawless, required that they put aside personal interests in order to render service in a time of need. Employees of the Water and Power Authority and the Virgin Islands Telephone Corporation, who are key to the recovery effort, are also to be lauded.

Special thanks is due to radio station WSTA. True to its name, we were "lucky" that, unlike all others in the electronic media, there were able to stay on the air. During the darkest hours of the hurricane, the voices of Lee Carl, Addie Ottley and others were the nexus that kept the territory together. Like ABC Niteline, hosted by Ted Coppel, which developed a life of its own beyond the coverage of the hostages in Iran, it is left to be seen whether "Lucky 13" will hold its new 24-hour format and emerge with a greater market share.

We would be derelict in duty if we omitted the countless individuals who pitched in once the hurricane passed to render aid to friends, neighbors and at the work place. Food, drink and even money were shared.

On these tiny islands, where, unlike yesteryear, some family members and childhood peers seldom, if ever, visit one another, behavioral patterns change suddenly, in the aftermath of Hugo.

People ventured forth to give assistance in the clean-up operations – clearing trees and debris from entrances and premises. Personally, I visited for the first time a colleague who was in distress after living next door for over six years. This goes to show that family and community solidarity tighten in the face of disaster. Though we may revert to old habits, we can never be the same again because of our mutual survival of Hugo.

Regrettably, there were some who failed to act honorably. They too tell us about ourselves since they are inescapably part of the larger whole. It appears that the vulnerability which the hurricane revealed showed that many were prepared to loot and prey upon those who had been weakened by the disaster.

These acts of vandalism are reprehensible and should not be condoned. However, referring to the perpetrators as "scum," "dirt" and other contemptible names is not likely to remedy such behavior, though such name-calling noticeably desisted after similar behavior erupted in South Carolina, after it too was hit by Hugo.

Rather, the fact that looting took place is cause for pause as we consider how is it that, in this paradise, so many among us seem to consider themselves outcast and are prepared to loot, actions that may very well be traceable to discontent with the social conditions that predate the hurricane itself.

Apart from the behavior of the hardcore criminal element, exasperated by the escape of inmates from the Golden Grove prison, it would seem that some among us, whether by virtue of their experience of relative poverty or whether on account of the contagion that goes with crowd behavior, consider themselves to be on the fringe of society. Such behavior suggests that they bear no allegiance and hold no sympathy for the territory.

If this be the case, to the extent that we wish to forestall a repeat of such actions, we need, going beyond the infusion of 1,200 "foreign troops," to carefully consider this issue because, if this group and sentiment should grow beyond its already disturbing proportions, the future of the territory seems grim indeed.

Hurricanes are far from being rare events in the Caribbean. Countries like Dominica, the Dominican Republic and, as recently as September last year, Jamaica have had their fair share of natural disasters and have been able to recover in good time without any permanent damage to their economies.

With federal assistance now at the disposal of the Gov. Alexander Farrelly administration, no less should be expected here. How well, Farrelly and his team, in the "politics of recovery", are seen to manage this crisis will influence their electoral support in next year's November election. So far, Delegate to Congress, Ron de Lugo's skillful actions have gained him many a vote.

Recovery from Hugo requires energetic leaders working closely with federal officials, banks, insurance companies, building contractors and many others. But in the final analysis, it is the resilience of the people, already in evidence, that determine how far and how fast the reconstruction moves forward.

The key psychological factor is that the people of the Virgin Islands must see the hardships as a temporary phenomenon and be made to feel confident, as spurred by their leaders, that the setback can be overcome.

Fire at SDA-run University
Is a Hurdle to Overcome

VI Daily News, May 12, 2012: 22 & 24.

F UNDAMENTALIST CHRISTIANS, INCLUDING Seventh-day Adventists (SDA), exhort one another and implore others to be on fire for God. However, the sudden and unexpected destruction of an auditorium at the University of the Southern Caribbean (USC) was a very unwelcome event.

The auditorium at USC is one of the key properties on the campus of this SDA-run institution of higher learning in northern Trinidad. It went up in a blaze, was engulfed in flames, and was gutted in a flash. This calamity is a terrific loss, despite insurance coverage. A figurative "Fire for God" refers to service to Him and proselytizing to the wider community on His behalf. However, this literal fire spelled disaster for the local and regional communities.

The SDA church is one of the fastest-growing Protestant denominations worldwide and many of its clergy; their support staff and others who hold positions in the government and the private sectors across the Caribbean are trained at this institution of higher learning.

The recent April fire, not the first (this was in 1973), is yet again one of the many setbacks that USC has faced over the years. It is undoubtedly the institution's newest hurdle in the way of its forward thrust as well as a test of the mettle of its relatively new-elected president, Dr. Clinton Valley, a Trinidadian, as well as for the constituencies it serves in Trinidad and beyond.

Though the cause of the fire could not be immediately determined, arson is suspected. However, now is the time for people of goodwill, including the government of Trinidad and Tobago, to come together and rally, with fervent prayer and other resources to assist in the recovery and restoration of the gutted edifice, its flagship and the venue of its graduation ceremonies and other special activities.

USC, with a current enrollment of over 5,000 students, from across the Caribbean and around the world, along with the Northern Caribbean University (NCU) in Manchester, Jamaica, are two institutions of higher learning in the Anglophone Caribbean that are part of the Adventist world-wide system.

Drs. Sylvan Lashley, a Barbadian, and Trevor Gardner, a Jamaican and the incumbent president of NCU, have served as top administrators of both of these schools. Occurrences, like the now memorable April 2012 fire at USC, formerly called Caribbean Union College, are catastrophes that are devastating in that they destroy the cherished buildings and other precious material objects of a people but never extinguish the spirit and courage to rise again like a phoenix to do God's biddings, shape minds for service toward Caribbean development and that quality of life espoused by Seventh-day Adventists and countless others.

Athniel "Addie" Ottley – Hero in the Face of Irma and Maria

VI Daily News, October 19, 2017: 19.

I‎T IS ALMOST impossible to compress the stature of truly exceptional human beings onto a printed page. Yet the feeble effort should be made so as to record the emerging consensus as well as register a society's acknowledgement of the need to pay due tribute.

It is commonplace and part of the human condition that we are disinclined to recognize the contributions of men and women while they are alive. We tend to nostalgically recall their involvement in events that have influenced the course of our lives only after they have transited and are no longer able to appreciate such gestures. Some contend that there should be no rush; we should allow time to pass; inquire of any possible hidden agenda and self-serving so that we can see clearly and not go overboard.

But infrequently the contribution of a man or women is of such magnitude; so compelling that there is no alternative but to respond to the inevitable and recognize a life of dedicated hard work over a long period of time in search of a better quality of life.

That is why, in the aftermath of the 2017 twin-hurricanes of Irma and Maria, the announcement to honor radio and other media personality Addie Ottley has met with such widespread approval locally and beyond. Sitting governments and the leaders of non-governmental institutions often make decisions to reward their cronies or the favored few. However, the decision to recognize Addie Ottley, a former Lieutenant Governor and opinion leader in the Virgin Islands, has met with universal approval. His name-recognition and acceptance rating far surpass that of any politician or CEO of any kind. His most avowed opponents or detractors will have to concede, even grudgingly, that high honor is most deserving.

No wonder that a broad cross section of residents in the Virgin Islands has stepped forward to unhesitatingly offer thanks, many in a tangible way, to this truly illustrious son of the soul for the magnificent and singular role that he and his family-owned and operated radio station, WSTA 1340, located in Crown Bay, St. Thomas, played during the 2017 hurricane season. This outpouring of support for Addie Ottley and WSTA is the people's attempt to show their debt of gratitude for a job well done.

All the other radio and TV stations that routinely service their listening and viewing audiences across the US Virgin Islands did not withstand the destructive fury of the wind and rain of these record-breaking hurricanes. They were knocked off the air and remained silent during the critical period long after the hurricanes had come and gone. Moreover, not only electrical service, but at a time when land-line telephone service was non-existent; the little internet connection was sporadic, resulting in isolation. WSTA was the only available communication nexus for everyone. This scenario included government, the private sector and all and sundry.

Hence, in the seclusion of homes and in shelters provided by government, bearing in mind the constraints of curfews hours, the calming voice of "Addie" as he is popularly known, served as a compass and tower of strength at a time of great trepidation, deprivation, disorientation and uncertainty, typical of conditions in the wake of disasters.

There are stories to be heard from the thousands of residents across the four-island territory, the British Virgin Islands as well, who made it through the stormy times and have had their lives changed for the better because of their connection in one form or the other to WSTA, a call-in radio station.

In an increasing competitive local marketing field, WSTA has its niche and, in the normal course of things, appeal to a more or less fixed segment of the population. One of its special offerings is the popular "Morning Show" when its host Addie, with his own inimical style; using the power of his personality, shows his craft with special features like "the Mystery Question" for a prize; the call-in happy birthday tributes, hallmarks of his ability to stay on top of things, past and present. His skillful and effective use of code switching between the dialect and standard English is his trademark and signature, along with his infectious laughter. With this repertoire at his disposal, it allows rapport with a broad cross-section of people. He can relate to both "the streets and the elites", a rear quality in colonial societies but the mark of the folk hero. This composite of traits is like magic and is woven into his ready-made commercials. His listeners and clients stay tuned and keep coming back for more from "the People's Station."

Then, there is his TV show "Face to Face" which, in an age of the dominance on global media, acts as a countervailing force in support of the local culture. Addie and his cohorts, especially his brother, Peter, with his apparent grassroots sensibilities, are without doubt standard bearers of the highest order.

But it has been proffered that along with the sterling record of the past as a communication veteran, including his wider involvement in the community, which includes religious affiliation as a Roman Catholic and active involvement in the Rotary, that Addie's center-stage role during hurricanes is the catalyst that has imbued him with hero status. This was true in Hugo in 1989, Marilyn in 1995 and now again in Irma and Maria in 2017.

Crises can bring out the best in all of us as borne out by the widespread positive perception of WSTA after hurricanes. These have further catapulted Addie Ottley into the public spotlight and underscore the role he played with dedication and commitment, far beyond his prior and regular diehard listening and viewing audiences.

Clearly, these circumstances, intersecting with his gifts and style, have stood Addie Ottley, WSTA and the Territory of the U.S. Virgin Islands in good stead. He is well deserving of honor and may have earned the status as the hero of the hard times associated with Hurricanes Irma and Marilyn.

An unheralded and impromptu night time telethon on WSTA is one of a number of campaigns that have been unveiled in response to an impassioned plea to help and give back to the struggling radio station. One grateful hurricane survivor, part of the groundswell and outpouring of appreciation and support, poignantly uttered "Even though I lost my roof, I still want to give X amount of dollars as a show of thanks to the radio station who was there for me in my hour of need." For those hampered by the violent hurricanes, Addie remain an unmatched voice of reason, guidance and hope.

We shudder to think what the circumstances of the next hurricane in the Virgin Islands would be like without WSTA and its lynchpin Addie Ottley. Hence, it is hoped that he will be afforded many more years when his energy, capacity for service and towering presence as a mass media figure will be at our disposal.

As a progenitor, it will be particularly important to have his insights available to us and succeeding generations as we are told by the well-reputed atmospheric scientists, including those who predicted that Irma "was a perfect storm", that in the future, Category 5 hurricanes will become the new normal.

X

Aging, Retirement
and the Afterlife

Virgin Islanders Can Live Longer and Better

VI Daily News, June 15, 2018: 23.

T HE NUMBER OF elderly people is increasing rapidly. People are
having fewer children and seniors are living longer. Our Virgin
Islands (like many countries, near and far) are becoming grayer and
grayer. Being an elder (elderly and old can be pejorative terms) is a
category open to everyone. It was estimated by the 1991 US Senate
Special Committee on Ageing that 80 million people in the U.S. will
be over 65 by the year 2030. The trend is the same worldwide.

No matter how well tuned we keep our bodies, the parts eventually
atrophy: bones and joints show varying levels of wear and tear, and
lead to problems like arthritis; they become more brittle, so injuries
take longer to heal. The odds of developing chronic illnesses (such as
hypertension and diabetes) increase. One or more of the five senses –
taste, sight, touch, smell and especially hearing – become impaired; less
sharp with age; the hair drops out, nails thicken and the skin wrinkles.
Hormone levels decline, usually causing physiological changes; the
immune system weakens and individuals are more prone to attack from
pathogens; the reproductive and urinary systems malfunction.

Though health becomes more fragile with advancing age, most elders
are not disabled by their physical condition. No more than 1% of elders

are bedridden. Of course, some elders have better health than others. Health problems are more common over age seventh-five.

In the psychological realm, the knack of learning new material and thinking quickly declines. However, the ability to apply familiar ideas holds steady with advanced age, and on average the capacity for thoughtful reflection and spiritual growth actually increases.

Physical decline is normal and inevitable among people in all age groups. However, there are significant differences between the elders. The young-old (ages 65-74) typically live independently with good health and financial security; they are likely to be living as couples. The old-old (ages 75-84) are more likely to have health and money problems and to be dependent on others.

The oldest-old (ages 85 and older), who usually require assisted living, know that death is imminent – it may come in a few months or in 15 years. An increasing number in this category are becoming centenarians, people who are 100 years old and older.

Centenarian status is based on genes and social class but mostly life-style. We can't change our genes, or often our social class, but we can live longer and better by changing our life style. Society usually defines old in chronological years. In the US, people are typically old at age 65, 66 or 67 because they can retire and become eligible for Medicare and full Social Security benefits. However, age is largely a social construct and, despite how we look in the mirror, our identity can come from within and how we feel.

Hence, elders are defining old age as coming later. Women generally live longer than men. They are more likely to seek medical attention and to work fewer years in stressful jobs.

Men generally die younger because of risky and unhealthy behavior; higher rates of cigarette smoking, heavy alcohol consumption and risk-taking in recreation and automobile driving.

We confront change at each stage of life. Being an elder has its rewards, but of all the stages of life's course, being an elder presents the greatest challenges.

Elders recognize that their lives are nearing the end, and the key to successful aging lies in keeping personal integrity and self-confidence while accepting growing old. People who remain active, physically and mentally, find the greatest satisfaction in life, even though their pace may be slower.

Physical Exercise. This can be our anti-aging medicine. As we pass 30, our levels of human growth hormone (HGH) begin to fall dramatically as our lifestyles become increasingly more sedentary. This is part of what influences the process of aging. However, exercise increases the production of HGH and the higher your level of HGH, the healthier and stronger you are going to be and the longer you will enjoy robust health and strength.

Exercise increases blood and oxygen flows to the brain, which, in turn, cleanses the body of impurities and decreases the risk of disease and cancer. Exercise releases endorphins, which give us a feeling of well-being.

To maximize exercise benefits, we must watch what we eat. A diet that includes fruit, vegetables, whole grains, and nuts, while avoiding food that contains saturated fats, is healthy at any age. Well before we reach 65, fat concentrates around vital organs and increases the risk of disease.

We need to get good-quality sleep, drink lots of water and optimize Vitamin D levels with lots of sunshine. When we watch our diet and exercise, we age slowly.

Mental exercise. The brain is like a muscle that grows stronger with use. You can keep your brain fit by engaging in behaviors that increase thinking, such as playing board games like dominoes, playing musical instruments, doing crossword puzzles and reading.

Social networks. Anxiety is the enemy of longevity, and although being alone at any age can cause anxiety, isolation is most common among the elders. Loneliness becomes a big issue. Family, friends and significant others may die or live far away and are unable to travel and visit. Isolation from people with whom they can truly share can lead to depression. Retirement closes off one source of social interaction, but "older people" still have the need to share thoughts and creative outlets. Joining clubs in line with one's interests enhances personal satisfaction and can not only reduce depression, but also lower blood pressure (which reduces the risk of strokes).

One's ability to drive oneself is crucial for social engagement - to see friends, to shop; to go to church and attend sporting and other events - and is consonant with independent living. Hence, the inability to drive as freely as before is a game-changer that affects the quality of life.

While many of us would prefer to see the physician as little as possible, as we age it is better to be proactive rather than reactive when it comes to our health. Regular medical checkups are needed to detect problems before they arise and to monitor risk factors for future illnesses.

We are living longer but are we happy? In addition to loneliness and depression, another problem that that plagues the elders is dementia or the loss of mental abilities. The majority of older adults don't experience dementia, but its prevalence does increase with age, rising from 1 to 2 percent in ages 65 to 74, to up to 30 percent or more in ages 85 or older. The most common form of dementia is Alzheimer's disease, a progressive, degenerative disorder that attacks the brain and impairs memory, thinking and behavior.

Most people dread the thought of ageing. No one likes getting older but we must refuse to pretend that it's not happening.

Aging is the constant reminder that death is on the horizon. The awareness of the inevitability of death makes most of us anxious. That's why our work and pastimes can act as distractions and are efforts to suppress this anxiety, as we cope with aches and pains and wait for death.

There may be nothing that we can do to stop the aging process, but we can determine how we age. If we can maintain a healthy life style - engage in physical and mental exercises; control our diet and remain socially engaged - maybe our real age will be much less that our chronological age.

But whatever our chronological age, it is important to understand and accept the body as it goes through the various stages of ageing. Accept the person that you have become.

Retirement Requires More than GERS and Pensions

VI Daily News, May 2, 2018: 21.

I N THE DEMOGRAPHIC profile of a country or territory, there are usually two vulnerable categories — children and the elderly.

Children usually have the benefit of a parent or parents to assist with their upbringing and survival— if not they may become wards of the state through age 18. Adulthood commences, and most aspire to contribute to society by becoming active working members. However, growing old or aging is insidious and as the years catch-up with the best of us, retirement ensues. Who will take care of us then?

Perhaps the Biblical advice to care for the aged as they cared for the young was readily obeyed in days of old. Today, however, there is an increasing number who are abandoned by young relatives and left to fend for themselves.

But as economic hardships increase, migratory patterns result in social distances between children and elders, making it even more difficult for many children to reciprocate and provide that cushion of comfort for their loved ones when needed.

Despite the many laudable examples around us, too many people are under the impression that "somebody" or their children will provide for them as they age. The Government Employees Retirement System and

Social Security often do not compensate for deficiencies in this regard and may add hurt to disappointment.

A major part of the solution to the exigencies of aging and retirement — in hopes of avoiding surprises, disappointment, and rancor when the "sunset days" begin – is to be self-reliant and to plan ahead. Unfortunately, this often is not a priority.

Whereas society pays much attention to preparing for the start and duration of work, it pays too little attention to the cessation of careers and the ushering in of retirement. The prudent thing, therefore, is for individuals to prepare as carefully for retirement as they do for their careers.

In the incipient years, particularly, in the heady excitement of youth and after settling into one's career or occupational path, few think about their old age despite its inevitability. It is interesting how reticent we are toward actively preparing for old age, when on average we are projected to live until 79, if not longer, especially given the increasing advancement in medical technology.

The retirement age can represent – after childhood, youth and adulthood— a period of time to be actively lived. What used to be termed a "short autumn of life" before death can now become a delightful, enchanting summer.

Similarly, the word "retire' does not connote rest in all vocabularies. For some, it is a time that is as an opportunity to attend to unfinished business; take items off your bucket list; begin a new career, enjoy the company of a spouse and extended family, or even teach the younger generations about lessons learned and living fully.

Additionally, there are many areas where the retired can still serve and their abilities can continue to flourish, contributing their time and efforts to organizations and others in need.

Money is the biggest retirement concern most people have. So, having a clear picture of your future finances will go a long way in allaying your fears and putting your mind at ease. Unfortunately, some people do not start thinking about financial plans for retirement until they are just about to retire. We can avoid having retirement sneak up on us by making plans ahead of time. The sooner we start preparing and the more thoroughly we plan, the more likely we are to enjoy ourselves when retirement comes our way.

Planning a comfortable retirement in the 21st Century requires a more intentional initiative model. The old approach to the Golden years – in which at age 60 or so we went from working to not working, collecting a pension, spending our time on the back porch or at the beach - has become outdated. Now the standard of living we enjoy in retirement hinges not on just a pension plan, but also increasingly on how much we take advantage of existing investment options.

Statistics have shown that we are living longer, staying healthier on account of annual medical checkups and remaining more active after retirement. In short, retirement is a whole new kettle of fish that offers many new possibilities, but it demands more careful planning on our part to be able to take advantage of the myriad opportunities.

Depending too heavily on either your family or government to take total care of you in old age is an insecure basket in which to put vulnerable eggs. In an age of economic recession, one's pension likely will not be enough as the cost of living rises, and the dollar buys less.

At a minimum, formal education for work generally takes place in the first 15 to 20 years. There is an average span of 40 or so years of gainful employment in which to prepare for retirement. Surely, we become so preoccupied with the demands of the workplace to ensure job security so that we can have the best life possible up to 65. But, along the way, it behooves us to devote thought, time and energy to how we will make it beyond that landmark.

Financial security does not just happen. It takes planning, commitment, paying attention to details and money. Putting away money for retirement is like you are giving yourself a raise. It is money that gives you freedom when you need it and deserve it most.

Retirement should be a cherished and valuable period, a time to fulfil ourselves with that which pleases us most; a time to use our knowledge and skills to the best advantage and embrace what Abraham Maslow termed "self-actualization."

However, unless proper preparation is made, old age and retirement can be a burden and even an albatross around our necks, rather than the best years of our lives. If we prepare well, then it can be said in earnest, "I have fought the good fight, I have kept the faith and finished the course."

DEATH AND ITS AFTERMATH

VI Daily News, September 22, 2018: 19.

MISTAKEN PUBLICATIONS OF obituaries are rare but do occur. One such case was that of Mark Twain who reported that his death was greatly exaggerated. It did eventually come for him in 1910.

Sigmund Freud once remarked that no man could truly visualize his own end. It is something that happens to others. We acquire a necessary blindness to death in order to function and live a more comfortable human existence.

Death is extremely disconcerting business. It would be bad enough if it simply lurked somewhere far in the future. But it constantly finds ways to insert itself into the lives of the living. It is a common end that awaits us all. Hence, we live with the numinous certainty that death with come.

People die as a result of a variety of reasons: natural causes, fatal accidents, disease, complications of old age and abuse of the elderly. In fact, as we get older, death is really a race between the various physical problems we face. Usually, life is lost by the one problem that will kill us first. The Christian premise is that fundamentally we die because of sin – "The wages of sin is death."

Regardless of the cause of death, few people give careful thought to their own demise. However, good stewardship should include our calculation of the financial cost of a funeral/farewell and burial or even cremation – all in keeping with responsible budgeting. Also, a will or trust can spare surviving relatives, the ones we love best, much less worry and headache.

Mothers are our first and most influential contact with social life, and because we love so deeply, we deeply feel the sorrow when the time comes for us to say our last good-bye. Losing loved ones is one of the most sorrowful experiences of life. It is something that no one relishes but everyone will have to cope with some time in life. Grief is the emotion that people feel when they experience a loss. It takes time and the healing usually happens gradually.

Participation in the viewing and funeral services of the deceased helps those who are grieving to get through the first few days as well as honor the person who has passed. It is important for those who have lost a loved one to express their feelings; it helps to acknowledge and admit that the lost has really occurred. Those who grieve should take care of their health and be sure to get plenty of rest. When grieving, seek out caring people – find relatives and friends who can understand your feelings and lost; rely on your faith, if you have one; take comfort that death, you believe, will ultimately be destroyed. Writing and offering a tribute can often seem like less of an ending and more like the beginning of precious memories that will last forever.

The Latin phrase "De Mortuis nihil nisi bonum" suggests how circumspect we are. "If here is nothing good to say about the dead say nothing." There is even the tendency, both in tributes and on epitaphs, to sentimentalize and cherry-pick the qualities of the dead – to gild the worse sinner with qualities never legitimately possessed, perhaps in an effort to erase or suppress painful memories or disappointments that he or she may have caused when alive. The dead are presented as normative characters in formal settings.

Most societies have a belief in life after death as part of their tradition. Some assume that their ancestors live in the skies or in heaven; remain in the grave, or inhabit some far off idyllic land. In line with this thinking and in response to the sudden death of 22-year old rapper sensation Mac Miller, Elton John exclaimed: "Wherever you are, I hope you're happy now."

Others even go further to ensure the dead ascend to utopian bliss. There is a second-chance while in the grave. Purgatory, as practiced by Roman Catholics, but not generally shared by other branches of Christianity, is a temporary stage of suffering and purification for believers, prior to going to heaven. All those in purgatory will eventual go there.

After death, the individual can experience purification so as to achieve the holiness necessary to enjoy the joy of heaven. For example, the novena – a nine-day cycle of masses to pray for the deceased individual. Detractors say that this implies that Christ's full payment for sin by His death is not sufficient, that it is too late to add works to the equation.

Cultures everywhere have shown some degree of preoccupation with the question of death. Humans have never wanted to accept their own finitude and have repeatedly created conceptions of an afterlife in order to disavow that life must end. It should come as no surprise that three of the world religions, namely, Judaism, Christianity and Islam, all adhere to the afterlife and the two-sided judgment that ensues. Hinduism, the oldest of them all, teaches that in the ongoing cycle of death and rebirth, the individual will get what he or she desires.

Religion has been the only institutionalized means whereby human beings have sufficiently grappled with their own mortality. In fact, for all the good that has come in its wake, the question of death is largely off-limits to science. No matter how successful science becomes in explaining, predicting and controlling the empirical world and enhancing the quality of life, science is powerless in the face of an unempirical concern like death

However, according to Harvey Cox, and as is most noticeable in contemporary Europe, "the world looks less and less to religious rules and rituals for its morality or its meaning."

In direct contrast, the Western Hemisphere, including United States, does not seem to be on the road to widespread and unfettered secularization. "God is not dead" and the claim that religion is declining may be off the mark, particularly in the Bible belt in the southern US. In the Caribbean, including the Virgin Islands, Judaism maintains a presence; there is a church of some kind almost at every corner; Islam is gaining ground among the youth; Hinduism is holding its own among East Indians in places like Guyana, Trinidad and Tobago and Suriname, and Rastafarian ritual is making inroads everywhere.

Moreover, the vast majority of people in the Western Hemisphere, including the United States, still say they believe in God. Actually, more people claim to pray each day than vote in national elections. Religious affiliation is actually proportionately higher that it was in 1850. And one of the most watched movies in recent years was Mel Gibson's 'Passion of the Christ,' which portrayed the final days leading up to the crucifixion of Jesus. However, belief in the afterlife has declined.

This turnaround is in part because it is difficult to appreciate and articulate the Kingdom of God or the afterlife to the post-modern mind, which is void of the sanctified imagination. This language sounds utopian. People are increasingly concerned with this earth and with this present life; they are largely materialistic; interested only in the reality they can see and enjoy now. Unlike the recent past, they are less interested in a vague kingdom, located in heaven that will be established in a faraway place.

Secularism, whether in its incipient or more advanced stages, eliminates other-worldly language from human discourse. When H. G. Wells was asked by a friend if he believed in another life, he replied "one life is quite enough." Like the theoretical physicist Stephen Hawkins who passed in 2018: "*They* don't believe in anything like heaven." As Mike Erwin wrote in defense of Hawkins "Nobody really has graduated to a place where an old white man with a flowing beard presides over a paradise."

The concept of the immortal soul that survives the death of the body and the idea that at death the soul goes off to another realm of conscious existence, in one form or the other, is one version of the afterlife construct – "Absent from the body; present with the Lord" is one of the supportive arguments used by adherents of this view. The ancient Egyptians imagined that their spiritual beings could survive their bodies and go into the heavens where they would become gods. Later, Greek philosopher Plato elaborated on the philosophy of the immorality of the soul (not subject to death). The soul, for Plato, existed apart from the body. This thinking that humans are born with an immortal soul has influenced traditional Judaism and some strands of Christianity

A competing strand of belief among Christians is that the body and soul are not separate existent entities but integrated; what affects the body affects the soul. It is the combination of body and the spirit/breath that make up a human being. Both body and spirit are required for human life to exist. Without one or the other, life ceases.

There is no conception of a future life after death without the involvement of the body. Hence, believers who have died will be resurrected with a body. Without a body, they have no existence. Moreover, after physical death, immortality is conditional.

The Christian bias is that those who have lost loved ones to death are to be comforted with the knowledge that when Jesus returns, those who have fallen asleep (not already in heaven), will be raised from the dead and given new, incorruptible bodies. Death is seen in terms of resurrection, not the immortality of the soul. It is an unconscious sleep from which we must be awoken in the resurrection.

Some act as if the here and now is all there is. For most atheists, the afterlife is a hypothetical and is not seen as part of one's destiny. At death, one's dreams turn to ashes. According to Emile Durkheim, religion, a universal feature of human existence, is man-made; a response to forces that human beings cannot understand but gives meaning to life; serves as a form of social solidarity and control, including emotional support.

Karl Marx, the materialist, sees it as "the opium of the people" and a form of false consciousness.

Everything human changes, fades and passes away. The Afterlife story has always been under pressure and debunked by skeptics who doubt its existence. If it is true that when we die the afterlife doesn't exist, it doesn't matter. However, if we conduct ourselves as if it does, we have everything to gain – eternal life.

Printed in the United States
By Bookmasters